Books
by Richard Roberts

TAROT AND YOU (1970)

TAROT REVELATIONS (1979)
with Joseph Campbell

TALES FOR JUNG FOLK (1983)

FROM EDEN TO EROS (1984)

THE ORIGINAL TAROT AND YOU (1987)

THE WIND AND THE WIZARD (1990)
in two volumes

SAVE THE WHALES

© RICHARD ROBERTS, 1991

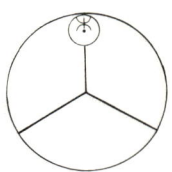

**VERNAL EQUINOX PRESS
BOX 581
SAN ANSELMO, CA 94979**

*This book is dedicated to
all our cetacean friends,
living and dead*

Library of Congress Cataloging-in-Publication Data
Richard Roberts, 1941 -
       Save the Whales
p.   cm.   91-65475
ISBN 0-942380-12-6   CIP

1. Whale and dolphin communication
2. American Indians
3. Mythology - American Indians
4. Joseph Campbell
5. Birds - Chickadees
6. Artist - Andrew Annenberg

TABLE OF CONTENTS

SCREEN TREATMENT

TITLE: "SAVE THE WHALES!"

CHARACTERS

THE PROFESSOR - A college zoology professor

DICK MELVILLE - A student

THE PRESIDENT - Of the Atlamtean Parliament

THE STORYTELLER - Of Atlamtis, 65 million years ago

A WOMAN - A citizen of Atlamtis, 65 million years ago

A MAN - A citizen of Atlamtis, 65 million years ago

THE AUTHOR

KAH - An Hawaiian, grandson of a Kahuna.

ROD and MARINA - Directors of the Atlantis Dolphin Center

PHIL and LOUISE - Wealthy benefactors of the Center

ANDREW and ARDATH - A visionary painter and his manager

THE DOLPHINS - Father, mother, son, and cousin; Darby and Joan.

A TUNA BOAT CAPTAIN AND HIS CREW

RATAVA - An enigmatical Indian.

Note: The two spellings above (Atlamtis and Atlantis) are both correct.

EXT. PLANET EARTH - DAY
A flying saucer descends on an ocean, whereupon the craft becomes
a ship propelling itself towards shore. Upon reaching shore, portals
open in the craft, which is called a pod by its occupants, two-legged,
two-armed creatures resembling humans in form except for bald,
high-beaked foreheads which jut out from the cranium. As they walk
out on ramps opening out from the pod, accompanied by wheeled
vehicles, we see that the shoreline contains a rich variety of vegetation, much of it unlike anything on earth today. Amid this lush
growth moves a wide array of animal life, dominated by many forms
of dinosaurs, the most terrifying of which is *Tyrannosaurus Rex.*

MONTAGE OF DINOSAUR CAPTOR AND PREY.
CLOSE SHOT - A small, shrew-like animal clinging to a broad leaf
high up in a tree, blinking down at the furious combat of the giants
below. SOUND OF THE PROFESSOR'S VOICE COMMENCES.

PROFESSOR
At this time in our evolutionary history we were tiny,
shrew-like, tree-dwelling creatures, probably surviv-
ing because we were too insignificant, that is, not
much of a mouthful for a dinosaur.

MONTAGE OF LAST VEHICLES DISEMBARKING FROM THE POD
accompanied by the pod's creatures. The ramps then retract into the
pod, and the creatures wave farewell as it moves out from shore,
gradually gaining speed until it becomes airborne once more, as the
heads of the dinosaurs turn to look, their eyes blinking un-
comprehendingly.

DURING THIS MONTAGE, SOUND OF THE PROFESSOR'S VOICE
CONTINUES

PROFESSOR
A pronounced gap in our history of dolphins and
whales is the absence of a fossil record of their extinct
sub-order *Archeocetes*, from the Latin *cetus* for whale,
and *archeo*, meaning ancient. Because of the lack of
any fossil record, it is impossible to even speculate on
how they evolved from a land-dwelling, air-breathing
mammal such as ourselves. They remain to this day
a mystery wrapped in an even greater mystery; for

1

they are removed both in space *and* time from ancestors known to us, and removed even from all the animal groups with which we are most familiar.

INT. CLASSROOM 1990 - DAY
VERY LONG SHOT
AS SOUND OF PROFESSOR'S WORDS ABOVE NEARS CONCLUSION, we are looking down from a very great height on the classroom as seen without a roof.
CAMERA DESCENDS RAPIDLY, CONCLUDING IN CLOSE SHOT of the Professor and— in the immediate background— the blackboard on which he has drawn the history of man and cetaceans.

MEDIUM SHOT
A student named Dick Melville raises his hand.

> MELVILLE
> Since you say that there is no fossil record of the whale's progenitors, could it be possible that they came to earth in spacecrafts of some kind?

> PROFESSOR
> I'd like to remind you, Mr. Melville, that this is a *science* class, and not a course in science-fiction.

> MELVILLE
> But if there is no fossil evidence, there is an outside possibility that their presence on the planet can be explained by extra-terrestrial origins.

> PROFESSOR
> Speculation like that will practically guarantee your repeating this course next year.

> MELVILLE
> Grant me this, without fossil evidence of any ancestors here on earth, then extraterrestrial origins are still a possibility.

> PROFESSOR
> All right, I'll grant that is a possibility, but to my mind the only real scientific possibility is still uncovered.

That is, we haven't dug deep enough.

Laughter from the class.

                    PROFESSOR
                    (continuing)
          Now the most compelling question before us today is
          not their origins, but how to save the whales. Any
          ideas?

                    MELVILLE
                    (raises his hand)
          Stop killing them.

Laughter from the class.

SLOWLY THE CAMERA PULLS IN TO the Professor's chalk drawing
on the blackboard of a whale, then CAMERA PANS RIGHT to where
there is only a question mark where the progenitor should be.
EXTREME CLOSE-UP OF THE DOT in the question mark.

EXT. EARTH - DAY
The beginning of the Tertiary Period of the Cenozoic Era, 65 million
years ago. The dot becomes earth as seen from high above, as from
a satellite or a spacecraft. Slow descent to a small island, ATLAMTIS,
which means SIT-MALTA in the language of the people living there.
SIT signifies position, posture, site; so the name literally means "the
site of Malta." Unlike our present language, their language is read
from right to left— thus Atlamtis. Malta's site then is as today,
directly south of Sicily, which is immediately south of Italy, the home
of Latin, which was to be influenced by this earlier language. In Latin
situs means position.

We see a building of unusual proportions that appears to be
rhythmically altering its proportions from time to time, and in and
out of this structure, like bees to and from a nest, move spacecraft
similar to that seen earlier in the arrival at the time of the dinosaurs.
Now instead of that primeval forest the island contains vast gardens
and orchards, including herbal plants of great medicinal and psychic
value, the seeds of which were brought with the creatures in their
spacecraft.

3

MONTAGE of shots of these creatures at work and play. They are very similar to those we saw disembarking from the spacecraft in the time of the dinosaurs; only their beaked foreheads have grown considerably larger. While at play, most of them are frolicking in the water at the beaches which surround the island. Others at work tend the many gardens; yet it is difficult to differentiate between one at work and one at play, because those working are as happy and creative as those at play.

INT. BUILDING - DAY
Inside, the same attitude prevails among these creatures. Enmity does not exist. They greet one another gaily, engaging in a challenging kind of game, a kind of multi-levelled verbal chess utilizing questions and responses, which are memorized and then called up again and resumed upon encountering another with whom the game was being played. The "game" has the effect of stimulating the neo-cortex of the brain, that area underlying the beaked forehead of these creatures, causing rapid growth biologically.

The building consists of many levels, most of them underground. A kind of musical sound is heard throughout, somewhat different on each level, but serving the same purpose of stimulating neo-cortex growth.

We pause on one level before a vast door, reading MUESUM GNIVIL. Our camera translates this for us immediately by changing the letters to read left to right LIVING MUSEUM. Inside are vast exhibits ranging from the now extinct dinosaurs to the Age of Mammals in the Cenozoic Era.

The trees within the exhibits sway as if to an invisible wind, and the fish swim freely.

MONTAGE of specific scenes within the exhibit, and the Atlamteans viewing the scene or passing by.

INT. ATLAMTEAN PARLIAMENT - DAY
Far larger than Britain's House of Parliament or the Senate in the U.S., it rivals the Colosseum in Rome. At least a thousand Atlamteans are seated there as their President begins his speech in a series of high-pitched vibrations resembling the sound of modern-day dolphins. A sub-titled English translation is given.

4

PRESIDENT

I come before you today, not as your President, but as one who like yourselves has been concerned for what seems to be a very long time with the matter of our future here on this planet, and the quality of our lives in that future, to the matter of which you have asked that this parliament be convened in order that all our voices be heard, if need be, and a decision arrived at today, if we are in agreement.

The first problem which we shall address now is that of the food supply. Although we have turned this island into a veritable garden since our coming, we are all aware of the great length of time from seed to harvest, and hence the many, many days required for tending the crops. Although we have all divided these labors equally, without regard for status, many have complained about the time such tasks have diverted away from Mind-Play, the pure passion of our species; hence in seeking to seed this planet we have somewhat stunted our own growth, since the neo-cortex of our brains grows proportionately to the amount of Mind-Play exercise given each brain.

Now although we have considerably accelerated the rate of growth of this island's vegetation, in order to suit our own agricultural requirements, unlike our source planet's higher atmospheric concentrations of carbon dioxide, which yields growth factors ten times that of this planet, considerably more technological interference with this planet's natural ecology would be required on our part, yielding only slightly more time for Mind-Play. I need not remind you that on all of the seeding missions our species has undertaken throughout the universe, the cardinal edict has been that we interfere as little as possible with the natural evolution of the flora and fauna of the planet which we are seeding. Hence, we have lived for the many years since our coming on this one small island, and our collecting field trips for the Living Museum have not altered this planet's evolution. However, the more our technology dominates this Atlamtean landscape, the more our mastery over this planet asserts itself. This was not the intent of the Avatar, as we know from our scriptures. Rather through Play we create our world and our selves, as The One did in descending from spirit to matter. From this process we learn and grow even closer to the consciousness of our Creator.

Furthermore, we may one day face a crisis in the far distant future when we must kill other creatures of this planet in order to prevent ourselves from being ːilled by those same creatures. Since our coming we have eschewed eating flesh, and we survived the period— at the time of the landing of our space pod— when the great dinosaurs held dominion over the planet. Our projections, however, indicate that a tiny shrewlike mammal that existed then, will one day walk upon two feet, and as its hands are freed then to create and manipulate tools, given the violently aggressive tendencies of its developing brain, it may one day have the technological might to wage war upon us.

This remark brings a unanimous and loud gasp from the Atlamtean parliament.

PRESIDENT

Yes, I am afraid it is true! Then we would be faced with fighting or fleeing, and we do not know if we could flee at that time because no one can say for sure if the Mother Pod will reappear again.

This remark brings to his feet an Atlamtean who stands patiently awaiting recognition from the President.

PRESIDENT

I recognize our much honored Storyteller and Keeper of Myths.

STORYTELLER

Mr. President, your words surprise me. Is it not the central teaching of the Avatar that the One descends to matter and thence ascends to spirit?

PRESIDENT

Yes, indeed, that is all our belief, but who can say whether the Second Coming of the Pod would be in time to rescue us in our hour of need, or whether we would have to endure many trials and tribulations in the flesh before being taken up again. If you can speak with certainty on this, I know we would welcome it.

STORYTELLER
(nodding)
I understand. I cannot.
(sitting down)

PRESIDENT

Then let me present my proposal to you all. I have outlined the agricultural problems. A further source of irritation with this planet, which we have come to live with, is the high density of gravity. As air-breathing mammals, we move about with great difficulty. It is not possible to play the air-leaping-games which we read of in the history of our native planet and its light field of gravity. Falls from injuries have beset all but the luckiest here on this planet.

Increasingly I find more and more of you at the seaside, playing in the water. While in the water, the gravity of your body's weight is balanced by the water, hence you float.

Now, in a moment, I'm going to show you a computerized projection of what we would look like and what life would be like if we lived in the sea instead of on land.

This remark of the President brings gasps and a chatter of conversation from the Parliament.

PRESIDENT
Order! Order, please!

One woman rises and remains standing as the din dies down.

PRESIDENT
Fellow citizen, you have a question?

WOMAN
Would we be living in the sea all the time and no longer coming on land?

PRESIDENT
Yes, that is correct.

WOMAN
Well, I for one could not stomach swallowing the flesh of fish even if it meant starving to death.

There are loud cries of approval from some of the Parliament.

PRESIDENT
Bear with me a moment, please. Your objections have been anticipated by the Scientific Committee. The seas of this planet are rich in a food source which you have never seen in the Living Museum because it is microscopic. We give it the name of plankton. This food source floats near the surface of the many oceans of the planet; and since the area of the oceans far outnumbers that of the land, this food supply is by and large inexhaustible— provided the seas are never contaminated, killing the plankton. You won't have to catch it or fish for it, however, because it won't try to elude you.

Now let me begin by showing you the computerized projections prepared by the Scientific Committee.

The lights go down and slides of ever-changing forms are projected on the wall behind the President.

PRESIDENT
First, we see a replica of our present bodily forms. The mouth is used not only for the eating, chewing, and swallowing of food, but also for breathing air. Next we see a hole at the top of the head, or at the back of the neck, as our forms are tilted horizontally as they

would be in the swimming position.

Notice the arms shortening progressively to become fins, and the legs fusing— separate only where the feet had been— as a flipper.

Now comes the main advantage to this form and to life in the sea. Here you see a close-up of the inner mouth. Instead of large teeth, there are plates within the mouth, basically nets for catching the plankton which are caught when the mouth is opened while swimming. The tongue is now enlarged, and while pressing against the trapped plankton, they are tasted and filter down the throat. I'm sure you'll come to love plankton every bit as much as the fruit of our Ambrosia trees.

Do you get the picture then? You have only to open your mouth and you feed. No planting, no reaping, *all* time freed for Mind-Play.

A man rises to be recognized by the President.

MAN
But how would we *communicate* for Mind-Play? Speech underwater would be garbled.

PRESIDENT
A very good question, indeed. And that brings me to the second part of this presentation. These pictures show you the range of voices talking from whispers to shouts in the medium of air. Very inefficient, indeed. Now in the medium of water sounds can be heard for several hundred miles. Modification of our vocal chords to produce the optimum pitch and frequency needed would result in Mind-Play between hundreds of beings at the same time hundreds of miles apart.

Again, gasps are heard from the members of Parliament, and much chatter and laughter breaks out. When it dies down, one man rises to be recognized.

9

PRESIDENT
Yes, you have a question or comment?

MAN
I have a question. How are these changes in our bodies to be brought about?

PRESIDENT
Through genetic engineering beginning of course at the individual cellular level. We have the knowledge and technology to begin it now.

MAN
And how long would it take before all Atlamteans would be able to live in the sea?

PRESIDENT
Perhaps as short a time as one hundred years, or perhaps a thousand years. The plan would call for volunteers to begin the experiment, and the best doctors and scientists would retain their own forms for several generations in order to ensure that they could minister to any of the new species should unforeseen problems develop, whether of a medical nature or from some other species in the ocean.

Since we have cremated all of our species since arriving in the Mother Pod, once we were all living in the sea, there would be no fossil records of us whatsoever, and it would be like pulling up a ladder, so-to-speak, on ourselves, leaving no traces behind once timed charges had been set to go off in the future to destroy these very buildings and all evidence of our highly technological culture. In this way we would be fulfilling in the greatest possible way the admonition of the Avatar not to interfere with the natural evolution of the planet. And, I might add, these new sea-going forms would preserve our present abilities to communicate telepathically, and these abilities might indeed grow and be considerably enhanced as the neo-cortex grows in proportion to the greater amount of time spent in Mind-Play. Certainly we shall be able to explore alternate probable realities as a result of the neo-cortex expansion.

This remark produces a kind of religious awe in the persons of the Parliament.

PRESIDENT
(continuing)

Now in closing, let me present to you the negative side of the pretty picture I and the Scientific Committee have presented here. You must recognize that as soon as you lose your hands because of the genetic engineering that will change your form, you will no longer be able to manipulate machines, and it is machines that have made us a great technological culture, able to travel eons of time and space throughout the universe. Without machines we become mere animals again, extremely gifted animals, but without the power to manipulate our environment, and in the final analysis, therefore, helpless. Helpless against any disease, helpless against any change in the environment that might be life-threatening, helpless against any species that might seek to wipe us off the face of the earth. Ironic, is it not, that the newest and highest development of our technology will be utilized— if you so choose— to return us to a more primitive form unable to utilize any technology whatsoever?

DOLLY IN SLOWLY to the concerned faces of the members of Parliament, then SLOW DISSOLVE.

EXT. MEDITERRANEAN SEA - DAY
UNDERWATER SHOT OF RUINED MARBLE COLUMNS AND TERRA-COTTA INLAYS.
The scene should resemble the painting "Aqueous Atlantis" by Andrew Annenberg. A mature bull dolphin and his smaller son swim into view. SOUND OF HIGH-PITCHED SONAR from them, which is their means of communication. The meaning of these sounds is displayed in sub-titles.

11

CLOSE SHOT
                              SON
                    Father, why are we here?

CLOSE SHOT
                            FATHER
                    I wanted to show you our origins.

MEDIUM SHOT
                              SON
                    I don't understand.

                            FATHER
            Millions of years ago we lived on land like the men who
            hunt us now in boats.

                              SON
            How could we swim on land?

                            FATHER
            We did not swim; we walked like men.

                              SON
            Was man hunting us then?

                            FATHER
            No, man was a little furry creature then, living in the
            ground or up in trees, but he did have his bad
            disposition even then.

                              SON
            Why does man hate us, father?

                            FATHER
            Man does not know any better.

                              SON
            Isn't there some way we can convince him we mean no
            harm.

                            FATHER
            Many of us are trying today. Some are swimming with

12

man. And some let themselves be captured to try to teach man.

                    SON
What can we teach him?

                    FATHER
That he is killing the oceans and the creatures in them, and in so doing he will one day kill himself and all of Earth.

                    SON
Why can't he see that?

                    FATHER
He does not look ahead.

FULL SHOT
A giant sea-turtle swims into view, and the younger dolphin begins playing with it by gently tipping it upside down while swimming in circles around it. The mature dolphin swims in and out among the marble columns, dipping down occasionally to inspect the terra-cotta floors where they are exposed beneath the sands. SOUND OF STEVE KINDLER'S MUSIC "MYSTIC FIRE" ACCOMPANIES THIS MONTAGE. MANY OF THE TERRA-COTTA INLAYS CONTAIN CRYPTIC SYMBOLS WHICH MAY BE RECOGNIZED AS ANTECEDENTS OF GNOSTICISM AND ALCHEMY. MONTAGE SHOULD INCLUDE CLOSE SHOTS OF THESE SYMBOLS, which the mature dolphin appears to be studying while his son continues his sport. Presently the elder dolphin swims to the side of his son.

CLOSE SHOT
                    FATHER
How did the land come to rise from the sea?

                    SON
It was carried up from the bottom by a gigantic sea turtle.

                    FATHER
Good. You are learning well the myths of man. If man

continues as he is going now, we may be the only ones to tell them.

SON

Father, how did this place where we started from come to be underwater and all broken up like this?

FATHER

An earthquake. The land went down into the sea.

SON

Can we go back on land to get away from man?

FATHER

No, we can only move by swimming now.

SON

How did man become such a menace?

FATHER

Through the tools he made with his hands.

SON

Didn't we once have hands?

FATHER

Yes, we gave them up for flippers so that we could swim better in the sea.

SON

And we're stuck in the sea.

FATHER

As if we were in a gigantic trap, within which more and more of us and other cetaceans are being killed every year.

SON

Where did we come from before we lived on land?

FATHER

From the air, through the air for a long time, from

another place way up in the sky.

                    SON
          I want to go back there, father.

                    FATHER
          All of us do, son.

SLOWLY FADE OUT

EXT. ATLANTIC OCEAN - DAY
FULL SHOT
A school of dolphins is sporting on the surface. Underneath them is
a school of tuna which is following them. From the subtitled dolphin
communications, we realize that this is the pod of the father and son
dolphins of the previous scene.

MED SHOT
The family pod of the father and son dolphins.

                    SON
          Father, why do tuna like to swim under us?

                    FATHER
          Because they feel safer.

                    SON
          What will happen if I try to swim under them?

                    FATHER
          They will just keep going deeper. Remember, they
          breathe through gills so they don't have to come to the
          surface.

                    SON
          Father, why do I ask so many questions?

                    FATHER
          So that you can learn.

MOTHER

Junior, shut up so that we can use our sonar to find some lunch.

SON

How is lunch different from breakfast and dinner?

FATHER

Shut up, son.

MONTAGE OF DOLPHINS HUNTING AND EATING SMALL SQUID. The tuna circle, waiting for the dolphins to finish feeding.

FULL SHOT

The dolphin and tuna schools viewed from the deck of a ship. THE TUNA BOAT CAPTAIN AND HIS CREW are encircling the dolphins and tuna with a gigantic net.

CAPTAIN

We've pretty well got 'em now.

DAVE

There's an awful lot of dolphins with the tuna, captain.

CAPTAIN

(turning to another crew-
man)

Dolphins? I don't see any dolphins. Do you see any dolphins, Arnie?

ARNIE

Nary a one.

Dave looks away in suppressed anger, realizing that the captain intends to violate international laws that forbid netting tuna when there are a large number of dolphins present.

MED SHOT

CAPTAIN

(shouting)

Pancho! Take the speed boat and head off any fish

trying to get out of the gap before the net closes.

FULL SHOT
The dolphin school:

> SON
> I don't like squid, father.

> FATHER
> It's an acquired taste, son.

> MOTHER
> Shut up and eat your squid, Junior!

> COUSIN
> I hear man's engine— close!

> FATHER
> Yes!

The bull dolphin immediately begins to direct his sonar in different directions. Satisfied with what it has told him, he makes a decision.

> FATHER
> (addressing the dolphin
> school)
> Follow me.

The school sets out after him.

FULL SHOT
The speed boat on the surface. Pancho, the driver, sees the dolphins heading for the gap where the net has yet to close, and speeds to cut them off. The speed boat arrives first and the startled dolphins turn away.

MED SHOT
The bull dolphin stops as the others veer off and start back the other way.

> FATHER
> Come back!

Seeing that it is no use, he turns and swims rapidly after them. When he catches up to them, they are panicky, swimming in chaotic circles, while the tuna mill around among them.

> FATHER
> Listen, everyone! You must follow me out past the boat! Soon it will be too late! Now once again.

Mother and son begin to slowly follow him, pursued at a distance by the rest of the school. The tuna do not follow.

FULL SHOT
The speed boat has progressed down to the other end of the net. Pancho, the driver, lets the engine idle as he scans the scene. When he sees the fins of the dolphins heading towards the gap behind him, he accelerates in that direction.

CLOSE SHOT
The bull dolphin leading the way.

> FATHER
> Come on! Now is our chance!

The speed boat is on a collision course with the bull dolphin. At the last moment Pancho veers off the tail of the dolphin, and once more the pod balks and turns back away from the boat. Pancho stops and throws a stun grenade over the pod towards the center of the encircling net.

MED SHOT
Underwater among the pod. SOUND OF INCREDIBLY LOUD EXPLOSION. The dolphins are hanging motionless in the water, except for the son, who was further away from the epicenter of the explosion because he was closest to the father. The father swims back to him from the other side of the boat, which he had passed under before the explosion.

> FATHER
> Son!

> SON
> (weakly)
> Yes.

18

                    FATHER
    Can you swim?

                    SON
    I guess so.

The rest of the dolphins seem to be reviving slowly, as the father
swims to the mother.

                    FATHER
    You must try to swim.

                    MOTHER
            (weakly)
    Yes.

                    FATHER
    Go to the surface and take a deep breath, and the rest
    of you who can, do the same. Then you must follow me
    out of the trap. It is our last chance.

FULL SHOT
Bridge of tuna boat. The captain is scanning the scene with binoculars.

                    CAPTAIN
    Pancho's grenade brought most of the dolphins to the
    surface.

                    DAVE
            (angrily)
    I thought you said you didn't see any dolphins.

                    CAPTAIN
            (turning on him)
    By god, Dave, if you want a piss-ant job on shore, keep
    on me and I'll see to it that you never work another
    tuna boat again!

                    ARNIE
            (interceding, to Dave)
    Hey, man, there's nothing but money floating out

there. If we don't pick it up, another boat will.

                    DAVE
            (angrily)
You guys know we're not supposed to take any
dolphins in the net!

                    ARNIE
Ah, come on, Dave, the sea is full of them. Another
pod won't matter.

MED SHOT
Underwater. The pod has gulped air from the surface and revived
enough to once again resume their pursuit of the bull dolphin as he
seeks to guide them out of the closing trap. However, this time their
movement is lethargic, reflecting the lasting effects of the stun
grenade.

FULL SHOT
In the speed boat Pancho sees that they are once again making for
the gap in the net.

                    PANCHO
        Haven't had enough, huh? Okay, one mo' time!

He guns the engine, and heads to cut them off.

MED SHOT
Underwater. The bull dolphin is leading, but his pace is slowed
because he has to constantly turn and look back at the slowly moving
pod.

MED SHOT
Pancho's speed boat slicing through the water towards the lead bull
dolphin.

MED SHOT
Underwater. The bull dolphin.

                    FATHER
        Whatever happens, everyone keep going!

CLOSE SHOT
The speed boat on a collision course with the bull dolphin.

CLOSE SHOT
Underwater. The bull dolphin.

CLOSE SHOT
The speed boat. A second before the collision, the bull dolphin leaps clear of the water, slamming into the side of Pancho's head and upper body. He is knocked over the side as the boat spins crazily out of control. The bull dolphin falls back into the water, the other dolphins escaping as the net finally closes.

MED SHOT
Underwater. The bull dolphin swims to the pod, now safely outside the net.

                         FATHER
          All here?

                         MOTHER
          Yes.

                         SON
          Are we safe now, father?

                         FATHER
          Yes.

CLOSE SHOT
Pancho sinking down through the water, bubbles streaming from his mouth and nose.

CLOSE SHOT
Underwater. The pod.

                         COUSIN
          Human drowning!

The pod springs into action, swimming down to Pancho to buoy him up by pushing under his body. Soon they have him on the surface, where he coughs up a mouthful of water and begins breathing.

FULL SHOT
The bridge of the tuna boat. The men are all looking in the direction of where Pancho was knocked from the speed boat, as he surfaces surrounded by the dolphins.

                    ARNIE
          What in hell happened to Pancho?!

The captain focuses on the scene with his binoculars.

                    CAPTAIN
          Those god-damned dolphins have got him, that's
          what!
                    (handing the glasses to
                    Arnie)
          Here, take a look!

                    ARNIE
                    (looking)
          They're trying to eat him!

                    CAPTAIN
          Get me that rifle!

                    DAVE
          Dolphins can't eat humans.

                    ARNIE
                    (handing rifle to Captain)
          Get out of the way, Dave!
                    (holding Dave)

                    CAPTAIN
                    (shooting steadily)
          Try this you bastards!

MED SHOT
The pod around Pancho. They are supporting him with their fins. He has come around and knows what they are doing. The first shot rips into the head of the mother dolphin, the next two into the cousin's body. They immediately float lifelessly.

                    PANCHO
                  (shouting)
      No! No! They saved me! No! No!

The next shot rips into Pancho's chest, and he dies immediately.

CLOSE SHOT
The bull dolphin underwater.

                    FATHER
          Dive!

MED SHOT
The son follows his father. When they surface they are all alone, some three hundred yards outside the net and well beyond the range of the tuna captain's rifle.

CLOSE SHOT
                    SON
          Why, father?

                    FATHER
          Don't talk, son.

PULL BACK TO FULL SHOT AS THEY SWIM AWAY IN THE DISTANCE.
FADE OUT

INT. OUTRIGGER CLUB, HONOLULU - DAY
In the background is a view of the curving shoreline of Waikiki Beach, the high-rise hotels in the distance. The AUTHOR is seated at the bar drinking a beer. Beside him is the only empty stool at the bar. Intent upon reading some papers, he appears not to notice a tall, muscular Polynesian, KAH, who sits on the adjacent stool and orders a beer. After a time, the Polynesian observes that the author is reading about dolphins and makes a comment.

                    KAH
      Are you interested in dolphins?

                    AUTHOR
      Yes, I've just arrived from California and I'm brushing

23

up on the Atlantis Dolphin Center on Maui, where I'm
going tomorrow.

KAH

I'm from Maui, but I don't think I've heard of it.

AUTHOR

It hasn't been around very long.

KAH

What do they do there?

AUTHOR

From what I've read and heard so far, they've made a
breakthrough in dolphin/human communication.

KAH

In what way?

AUTHOR

They seem to be able to "call" the dolphins in to swim
with people.

KAH
(laughing)

My grandfather could do that, and his grandfather
before him.

AUTHOR

Oh? Well, I understand they also think they're on the
brink of deciphering "dolphinese." By the way, my
name is Dick Roberts.

KAH
(extending his hand)

My name has 26 syllables in Hawaiian so I'll spare you
that. My nickname is Kah.

AUTHOR
(shaking his hand)

Kah, pleased to meet you.

KAH

It's short for Kahuna, which means priest in English,
I guess, but a Kahuna is more like a shaman.

AUTHOR

Did you ever see your grandfather call the dolphins?

KAH

No, but my father did. Around the turn of the century
he was a young boy living in the Kalalau Valley on
Kaui where many Hawaiians still lived. On the western end, the valley opens to the sea. My father told me
the story so many times I'll never forget it.

AUTHOR

Was your father a kahuna?

KAH

Well, yes and no. He inherited the job, you know, from
my grandfather, but he never had the spiritual power,
or *mana*, like my grandfather. Mostly he made ocean-
going canoes, and the kahunas of old had many
specialties, you know, which they taught to others.
But when the war came, my father moved to Honolulu
with his family to work on ship repairs.

AUTHOR

From canoes to battleships.

KAH

That's right. In the old days, every job had a kahuna
overseer, so that things proceeded according to the
proper ritual. If the wrong tree was selected to make
the canoe, or if permission was not asked of the spirit
dwelling in the tree, you could drown in that canoe.
In the same way, there were kahunas who presided
over, you know, healing, agriculture, astrological
prophecy, architecture, fishing, you name it. The
kahuna who had the greatest knowledge in the most
fields, and the greatest *mana*, became Kahuna Nui,
the high priest and councillor who advised the king in
all matters and helped him run the government.

AUTHOR

Tell me the story of how he called the dolphins. Maybe it would be useful for the Dolphin Center to know about it.

KAH

I doubt that but here goes. Well, although fish were plentiful—and my grandfather could hold his breath underwater four minutes—about once a year the Chief of the colony living in the Kalalau Valley would urge my grandfather to call the dolphins in for a feast, usually on the Chief's birthday. The way he did it was this. He would go into his house and meditate, or go into a trance, my father was never sure which because no one was allowed to watch. But he said grandfather told him that his spirit would leave his body and go to where there was a school of porpoise far offshore. He would address them as "my friends from the West," and invite them to swim into shore for a great celebration with his people. There was a chant involved, which he had to get just right, or the porpoises would ignore the invitation. Once he had contacted them and they began coming in, which took many hours, he would rush out of his lodge crying, "Our friends from the West are coming!"

AUTHOR

Fascinating!

KAH

Now all the time he had been in his trance or meditation, the villagers were busy carrying out a huge deception. The women prepared elaborate meals, and the children made wreaths of flowers, and the men put on their feathered headdresses. Soon the dolphins' fins were seen outside the reef, and the villagers all ran into the water to help the porpoises over that part of the reef where it was too shallow for them to swim. The children splashed about in the shallower water playing with the dolphins, and everyone called out to them, "Our friends, our friends!" But at a given signal from the Chief, the men and women took out knives and spears and began slaughtering the dolphins while the children held their tails. Once they had all been killed, a big fire was ignited, and they barbecued the flesh. So the dolphins had been invited to a feast after all, but they were the dinner.

> AUTHOR
> Sickening! After that story, I'm not sure I'll be able to eat my dinner tonight.

FADE OUT

EXT. ATLANTIS DOLPHIN CENTER - DAY
FULL SHOT - A taxi pulls up and the Author gets out and is greeted at the door by MARINA DEL MAR and her husband, ROD.

> AUTHOR
> Hello, I'm Richard Roberts.

> ROD
> This is a pleasure. Meet Marina, she's one of your greatest fans.

> AUTHOR
> (shaking hands with Rod and
> Marina)
> Well, I thought the reason you invited me must have something to do with my books, because I know nothing about dolphins.

> MARINA
> It does, but come out to the pool and meet Darby and Joan.

> AUTHOR
> Darby and Joan, the great pair of lovers?

> MARINA
> Yes, they weren't together in the wild, but in captivity they have certainly become a couple.

CAMERA PANS with them as they walk towards the pool. We see that the pool adjoins the sea, and doors can be opened permitting access in or out. When the dolphins see the humans approaching, they swim to the edge of the pool, lifting their heads out of the water and greeting them with excited chirps and whistles.

> ROD
> Here is Joan and here is Darby.
> (Kneeling down at the edge of the pool he touches their beaks).

> MARINA
> Do you want to touch them?

> AUTHOR
> Oh, sure.
> (kneeling down, he imitates Rod's action)

> ROD
> Tomorrow you can swim with them if you want.

> MARINA
> For now, we have reservations for dinner at a local restaurant.

CUT TO

INT. RESTAURANT - NIGHT
The decor is nautical but nice. Rod, Marina, and the Author are seated at one table. From time to time during their conversation a waitress appears bearing new dishes of food, while carrying away empty plates.

> AUTHOR
> This is quite a feast.

> ROD
> When you said you liked seafood, we knew you'd like the Friday night specialty here.

AUTHOR

I do, but I'd also like to know why you invited me to be your guest at the Dolphin Center, because as I told you in my letter, all I know about dolphins is from reading John Lily. He was at Esalen back in the sixties and seventies when I used to go there with Joseph Campbell.

ROD

Joseph Campbell is another reason why you're here. I've read everything he's written, but never got a chance to attend one of his lectures when he was alive, and I'd like to know more about him.

MARINA

And I am particularly grateful for your book *From Eden to Eros: Origins of the Put down of Women.* Your chapter on "Nature, Body, Sex" told me that you are aware of the need for a special harmony between human consciousness and the natural world, and the cosmos.

AUTHOR

For want of a better name, I called it the "Vibrational Theory."

MARINA

You said, "The world is the natural extension of divine creativity and intent, lovingly formed from the inside out— so there was consciousness before there was matter, and not the other way around."

AUTHOR

Actually I didn't say that, Jane Roberts' Seth did, but I believe it, and I'm sure Joseph Campbell believed it.

ROD

That brings us again to why you're here. Our work has been primarily on the level of attempting to communicate with dolphins in order to create a common language, but we have found out that the dolphins are attempting to communicate with us!

MARINA

Not us personally, but with all humans. That is why all over the Hawaiian Islands they are swimming into shore when humans are there just to swim with them.

AUTHOR

Yes, I've heard of that. A grandson of a *kahuna* whom I met in Honolulu last night told me that they can be "called in" using a special chant.

ROD

We think now that they come in response to telepathic messages from humans, that is, just *thinking* about them causes them to want to come. The kahuna probably believed that it was the chant, but his *thinking* about them while chanting actually brought them in.

AUTHOR

But there are *millions* of environmentally conscious people today, why would you want me here?

MARINA

This is where it gets interesting.

ROD

Well, we *have* bridged the barrier of animal communication. *We* are being instructed by those two dolphins you saw in the pool, two high and mighty humans. This has not got out to the press or the rest of the world yet, but it's true.

MARINA

And one of the basic ideas they are telling us appears in your collaboration with Joseph Campbell, *Tarot Revelations*.

ROD

You have one chapter called "Alchemical Descent." In there you say that the basic premise of alchemy is that a spiritual essence interpenetrates matter. The One makes a vertical descent to earth, and the

30

spiritual and mundane, above and below, are joined. And on the next page you show a vertical numeral one, descending like an arrow to earth— above to below.
(drawing it for the Author)

AUTHOR
Yes, the circle with a single vertical line symbolizes salt in alchemy, which is basic matter, which spirit acts upon...

ROD
(completing the drawing
thusly)
...to form the symbol for Earth. Thus, as you say, the symbol for the mundane plane is compounded of the glyph for salt and the descended One.

MARINA
Some of the stuff we're getting from the dolphins is about the One descending to earth, but there is much excitement from them about ascending to the One.

AUTHOR
Upon dying or...?

MARINA
No, we're not exactly sure. That's where we hope you can help us.

AUTHOR
Yes, all this is in Jung's *Mysterium Coniunctionis*, which Joseph Campbell gave me, along with a whole crate of books from the Bollingen Foundation after Joe and his wife stayed at my apartment back in the sixties.

ROD
You mentioned in your book that was the weekend when you both discovered the Tarot.

AUTHOR

Well, I had only been given the cards the week before, but we tried a reading and found all the stations in the hero's journey turning up, so we both wanted to learn more about them. It has been said that if the twenty-two cards of the Major Arcana were arranged in the proper order, then their inner meaning would become transparent. When we both came up with an arrangement, that led to our writing the collaboration.

But let me back up for a moment, because I haven't the foggiest idea how a human and dolphin would communicate, so when you say you're getting from the dolphins certain ideas, how is that possible?

MARINA

Well, it all started with John Lily. He somehow recognized that dolphins were special creatures.

ROD

Without that insight on his part none of the work that came after— including our own— would have taken place.

MARINA

Dolphin communication centers have sprung up all over the world. In California there is the center for Marine Studies, run by Ken Norris and Chris Johnson, and in Honolulu Dr. Louis Herman has succeeded in getting dolphins to carry out commands given in sentences.

AUTHOR

How does that work?

MARINA

Well, he started by simply getting the dolphins to name objects by mimicking the trainer's speech. Once they knew certain objects, action combining them could be taught.

ROD

For example, FETCH BALL HOOP. The dolphin gets the ball and swims to the hoop, where it is pushed through. Then he gets a reward.

AUTHOR

Two points! Okay, I can see that kind of thing happening, but how can dolphins communicate things they have not been taught? That is, I assume you're not teaching them how to read Tarot cards!
(laughter)

MARINA

(laughing)
No, not yet.

ROD

What you have to realize is that whales and dolphins already have all the languages of all the earth's people in their heads, but the difficult thing for them is to communicate with us by means of human speech, because that is not their natural means of communication between themselves.

Take the whale's so-called "song." We have always assumed that it proceeds by linear progression, but instead it is more like a sandwich of meanings and transmissions.

MARINA

For lack of a better name, one could say that in the "inner ear" of the whale the song from another whale is stored.

ROD

And what is shared is not just a sound but also a vibration. Following sounds of the song may contain certain audio or vibrational signatures, which may themselves be stored in the inner ear, or they may trigger the playback of the earlier stored sounds, setting off the sandwich effect. Hence, the whale "hears" the song not entirely as it was transmitted, but in a highly intricate form which compounds the meaning of many levels.

MARINA

We have discovered from this that the whales and dolphins have myths just as mankind does.

AUTHOR

And have you found out all this from just your two test dolphins?

ROD

No, that comes from years and years of listening— and taping— the communications in the sea of whales and dolphins. Science has sought to decipher this electronically, like cracking a code, but Marina and I, and now you, know that we have been on the wrong track.

AUTHOR

Well, then how did you decipher these cetecean communications?

MARINA

Through a telepath. You'll meet him while you're here in Hawaii. He has transcribed an enormous amount of material from the tapes of the cetecean communications. Some of it is quite mystifying, even though it appears in perfectly good English. That's what we want you to look at, and also those transcriptions that have a relation to your books.

AUTHOR

I can't wait to see it.

ROD

If you'd like to stay a month or two, you can live at our house and come and go as you please at the Dolphin Center.

AUTHOR

Sounds great.

EXT. ATLANTIS DOLPHIN CENTER - DAY
FULL SHOT -
It is the next morning. Rod, Marina, and the Author are about to enter the building.

                    ROD
          (to Author)
     I'll get you a set of keys. In the meantime, be careful
     of this door. Once you're in the lobby you can't get out
     unless you have a key, or unless the door is propped
     open.

                    AUTHOR
     Why the security? Is there something of great value
     here?

                    MARINA
     You might say so.

                    ROD
     She means the painting.

                    AUTHOR
          (looking up to the painting)
     Wow!

                    MARINA
     Everyone loves it.

                    ROD
     It's called "Aqueous Atlantis."

MED. SHOT of painting. There are dolphins swimming among
marble columns, and two engulfed pyramids are in the background.
The size is 4 x 6 feet.

                    AUTHOR
     Who is the painter?

                    ROD
     Andrew Annenberg. He lives in Maui and mainly just
     paints dolphins.

AUTHOR
This is quite a vision. I feel as if I'm actually underwater.

MARINA
We're going to put on our suits now and go into the pool with Darby and Joan. Why don't you join us?

AUTHOR
Oh, great!

EXT. POOLSIDE - DAY
FULL SHOT - The dolphins are swimming excitedly and "clicking" in anticipation of the humans entering the pool. MONTAGE of Rod, Marina, and the author swimming with the dolphins.

FADE OUT

INT. RESEARCH ROOM OF DOLPHIN CENTER - DAY
Files running from floor to ceiling predominate. There is also a long table and half a dozen chairs. Two desks against the walls hold computers.

MED SHOT
ROD
Okay, all the material you'll be dealing with is in this one room. The *blue* filing cabinets contain all the deciphered transcriptions of *whale* communications from hydrophone microphones in the ocean. The *grey* cabinets hold the *dolphin* material.

AUTHOR
And you say this was all transcribed by one man?

ROD
Right. Ratava.

MARINA
He's in India now, taking a little holiday, but he should be back next week.

ROD

Incidentally, some of it is from Sanskrit.

AUTHOR

The whales were speaking Sanskrit!

MARINA

That's what we asked, but remember these transcriptions were deciphered not mechanically but
telepathically, so it was Ratava's sense of the meaning that it was Sanskrit.

ROD
(opening a file drawer and
pulling out a folder)

Here, this will give you an idea of how he's done it. At
the top of the first page of the transcription is the
name of the listening station, it's location, the date,
and then the language. Ratava knows French, German, Spanish, Greek, Latin, as well as English and
his native Indian language.

AUTHOR

Since there is so much material, I think I'd do best
sifting through the English transcriptions at first.

MARINA

That's a good idea.

ROD

We have made a duplicate file for you in which there
is material which you speak of in your books.

AUTHOR

Oh, marvelous. This is really exciting.

MARINA

We thought you wouldn't be disappointed.

ROD

But before you get to work, we have been saving our
best story. This happened about six months ago....

SLOW DISSOLVE TO

EXT. POOL AND DOLPHIN CENTER - DAY
CAMERA FILMS ALL THE ACTION SUBSEQUENTLY DESCRIBED
IN THIS SCENE.

                         ROD
                    (continuing)
Since the parking lot is on the other side of the
building, and there are no back doors there, I had
parked my car at the front lobby door in order to
unload some heavy supplies. Usually only trucks
park there, but this time it was necessary for me to
park there. I had to make several trips from the car to
the back rooms beyond the lobby. I hadn't paid any
attention to Darby and Joan, but when I went to close
the back hatch of the car, I noticed that they were
"standing" at the edge of the pool intently watching.
Dolphins can stand partially out of the water by
balancing on their tail and fins. After I parked the car
and walked back, I noticed that the dolphins were
very agitated, rushing up and down the pool, and
clicking back and forth to one another. Even though
our communication session wasn't scheduled until
later in the day, I said, "Okay, if you want to start now,
let's do it."

When we first started our training of their mimicking
human speech, we had to begin with the sounds of
the letters of the alphabet. On an underwater TV
screen in the side of the pool, a tape continuously
played each capital letter while a voice made the
sound of the letter, both above and below water. That
way the dolphins could play with it whenever they
wanted to. One thing we have found is that if you bore
them, they won't cooperate and will just swim away
from you. The continuous tape system worked very
well, and a week later they were able to recite from
memory the entire alphabet. Certain letters gave
them more problems than others, but that is true of
humans as well. I once knew a German who could not
say the letter "V," it always came out like a "W."

So because the dolphins were so agitated on this day, I decided not to postpone our session until the afternoon. I put on a training tape that used sentences to instruct them to carry out assignments involving two or three objects, which were in the pool or within their reach at poolside, but they wouldn't even look down at the TV screen in the side of the pool. Instead, they just stared at me. In order to break the monotony, I threw them two fish rewards even though they hadn't done anything. They didn't even look at the fish flying past their noses. Then I thought maybe they were sick, but rejected that idea at once because of their fleet swimming earlier.

They had been hanging back several feet from the poolside; now Darby and Joan came closer. They had trouble with "who, what, and which" and figuring out the proper ones to use in asking questions, so we came up with a shorthand sound for them to use which would indicate to us that they were asking a question. Darby made the sound, and Joan repeated it twice, and then he said, "Animals salve?" or so I thought. The sound was *sav*, and rhymed with have. Have was a word used a lot by us and them in the training sessions. "I have hot" meant, "I am hot." Or "I have ball," etc. "Salve," the word they were saying, means a healing ointment, and we sometimes applied a salve to their skins when they had a nick or scrape. Both of them were now repeating over and over, "Animals salve?" and I figured if they wanted medicine or aid they would have come within reach, but they stayed just beyond arm's length.

I couldn't figure out what was going on, so I decided to call Marina at the house. "Did you teach them the word 'salve'?" I asked.

"Of course not," she said. "What's going on there?"

I told her the story, but she had no more ideas than I did.

I went back out to the pool, and they started with a new question, "Not (or no) salve dolphin (meaning themselves)?" By this time I was hung up on the word "salve" and not able to see beyond it. If I had, the answer to the mystery would have been easy. But I decided they just wanted to play around and not work and said, "The hell with it."

I had to get something out of the glove compartment of the car. Walking around to the parking lot, as I approached the car, the first thing that struck my eye was my bumper sticker "Save the whales!"

Then it hit like a ton of bricks. That morning the dolphins had seen the bumper-sticker, and were asking me, in their first question, "Animals save?" "Which animals were humans going to save?" When I didn't understand that, they were asking me would I not save them? No wonder they suddenly saw me as a threat.

Running as fast as I could I sprinted around the building and leaped into the pool. Tears were flowing down my cheeks, and dolphins pick up a human's emotions before anything else. Despite the ambiguous message my bumper-sticker had sent to them, my love for them now was certain. I hugged them and we frolicked for what seemed like hours. I drove home in my wet clothes to a balling-out by Marina because I was half an hour late for a dinner engagement.

INT. SAME ROOM AS BEFORE AT DOLPHIN CENTER
CLOSE UP - MARINA

MARINA
The funny thing was we had been using the word "save" in some of our training sessions. But if they pronounced it sounding like "have," which they already knew, we didn't bother to correct them. We wanted them to mainly get the *meaning* of a word.

MED SHOT - Marina, Rod, and the Author.

                    AUTHOR
How did the word "save" come into the training?

                    MARINA
You've probably heard before of dolphins surrounding
a swimmer attacked by sharks. Like humans, they
are as a species epimeletic, that is, "care-giving." In
the pool, either Darby or Joan will "play dead" like a
dog. Then the command is given, "Save Darby," and
Joan will push him to the surface. It is in the sense
of "taking care of, keeping up, not letting die," that
they knew the meaning of the word "save." Of course,
"Save the Whales!" means *preserve* the species, but
on an individual level it means "support and not let
die" each and every one.

                    AUTHOR
             (to Rod)
So you got an education that day.

                    ROD
Did I ever!

                    MARINA
Incidentally, we call the speech of the dolphins "dolphin-say." Its the language they use in trying to
communicate with us.

                    ROD
Let's sit out by the pool and we'll tell you the story of
how the meaning of "save" took a theological direction
when we had a group of children come to visit from a
rather fundamentalist church school.

EXT. POOL - DAY
MED SHOT

                    MARINA
We must take your picture and put it on the TV with
your name above it so that they can learn to say your
name.
             (to the dolphins)

Name? Name?

FULL SHOT - The dolphins swim up to Marina and squeak out her name. She gives them each a fish.

                    ROD
We finally found out that it's easier for them to say "Rodney" than "Rod."

                    MARINA
Probably "Rich" would be easier than Richard, don't you think?

                    ROD
We can try "Rich" first and see what happens. I noticed when you were swimming with them that they really took to you. Sometimes people have some fears the first time, and the dolphins sense that and it puts them off, since they like human contact and have only good vibrations to put out.

                    AUTHOR
After thirty years of body-surfing I have no fear of dolphins. Now if you'd asked me to go into the pool with a trained shark, I might have some second thoughts. You started to tell me the story of how theology got into the act.

                    ROD
Yes, we often have groups of school kids visiting here, some from church schools.

                    MARINA
Mostly the kids just want to touch the dolphins and swim with them, but these kids wanted to convert them!

                    AUTHOR
To what?!

                    MARINA
Their way of thinking. They were *very* religious people,

even for kids.

ROD

They were telling the dolphins that their— the kids'—
souls were saved. Since that word "save" had created
so many problems on that famous day I just told you
about, naturally the dolphins later inquired of us,
"What means save soul?"

MARINA

Ratava told us that Darby and Joan had told him
telepathically that for all whales and dolphins there
was a "truth" that they had come from Above, and
that they would return Above after "body swims no
more."

ROD

Not too far removed from the Christian myth of the
Holy Spirit incarnating into the flesh and then returning to Heaven at death.

MARINA

Anyhow, the next week the kids from the church
school were back again, and the dolphins seemed to
remember them and their talk about "saved souls."

ROD

So the dolphins asked them, with a little help from us,
"Where go saved souls?" or, "Where are kept saved
souls?" The kids all shouted "Heaven, heaven!"

MARINA

We hadn't used that word before in dolphin communication. It wasn't part of dolphin-say, so Darby
and Joan were very perplexed. Then we remembered
the dolphin truth about Above, and explained "Heaven"
to Darby and Joan by substituting Above. Immediately Joan replied, "Same dolphin go." And Darby
nodded his head vigorously and repeated what Joan
had said.

43

ROD

This precipitated quite an argument among the children. Some of them were quite glad to know that there would be dolphins in Heaven, whereas some of the others began to spout scripture to the effect that only Man was endowed by the Creator with a soul, and, therefore, whales and dolphins would not be saved.

MARINA

However, one little girl called it "unfair," and said, "It's as if we were judging the dolphins."

ROD

There was an awful lot of screaming between the faction of kids who championed "dolphin-soul" and those who were hard-line Bible-thumpers, but eventually they were shouted down, and an official reply was prepared for Darby and Joan which went something like this. "Human, or man, has soul. Dolphins no have soul. Dolphins no can go Above."

MARINA

(laughing)

But Darby and Joan got in the last words. They replied, "Who says?"

ROD

The kids started screaming, "God! God!" at the dolphins. When they quieted down, Darby said in dolphin-say, "If humans have soul, why kill dolphins?" Joan nodded her head up and down very vigorously, and she and Darby swam to the opposite end of the pool and would have no more to do with the children, who promptly left.

MARINA

But that was not the last we heard of it.

ROD

That simple, unanswerable question from Darby and Joan, "If humans have soul why kill dolphins?" created a storm of controversy, because the implication was that mankind did not have a soul. All the centuries during which humans had slaughtered whales were now being thrown in the faces of the sanctimonious parents by their heretofore obedient children.

One day we got a call from the head of the church school who wanted to take me to task for what was going on. I explained "dolphin-say" to him and how it had come about, but he went right back to blaming me for the uproar between the parents and their children. I told him, "Look, I have no control over what the dolphins will say." His reply was, "If you're going to bother to train dolphins at all, at least teach them to be good Christians!" And with that he slammed down the phone. Needless to say, the children of that school haven't been permitted back here by their school principal.

MARINA
What happened in the following months boggled our minds to such an extent that we made none of it public, even falsifying our records so that it appeared that the training sessions were concerned with the practical application of dolphins serving man, in warfare, for example.

ROD
Obviously we feared losing funding, but beyond that our lives had changed as dramatically as if a chasm had opened up, propelling us headlong into a world we never dreamed possible.

AUTHOR
Why? What happened?

MARINA
In effect, our dolphins now began to teach us, but not so condescendingly as we had taught them, assuming them to be of a lower consciousness than our own. I use the word "consciousness" rather than "intelligence," because intelligence is measurable and

45

based on certain kinds of knowledge only. What our dolphins gave us was a lesson in metaphysics, showing us the limitation of our concept of the Creator and the universe. Rather than render this in dolphin-say, I'll give you the gist of it in plain English. First of all, whales and dolphins are not indigenous to planet Earth.

AUTHOR

Well, that explains why there is no fossil ancestor for whales and dolphins.

ROD

Precisely. "Then where did you come from, and how did you get here?" we asked them. "On a gigantic 'pod,'" was the reply. Now 'pod' means a school of cetaceans to us, but to them it also means the craft that brought them to Earth.

MARINA

As to the time in history when this arrival of the pod occurred, from their descriptions of the then dominant animals— dinosaurs— we can say that it was either the Jurassic or Cretaceous period of the Mesozoic Era.

ROD

One hundred and fifty millions years ago.

MARINA

Cur "lessons" from Darby and Joan were pretty slow and laborious until Ratava arrived to accelerate the process through telepathic communication. We would still depend upon our mutual language of dolphin-say, but if we were temporarily stumped by what Darby and Joan were trying to tell us....

ROD

...because not everything was in dolphin-say.

MARINA

...then Ratava would say a word that he got telepathically, and then they might nod their heads up and down in agreement, because they would be *receiving* telepathically from him the correct meaning they had in mind, even though they did not know the meaning of the sound of the word he was saying.

AUTHOR
In other words, when one learns to carry on a conversation, a meaning goes with the sound. The dolphins though, might not have the word in their brains, but Ratava could send the meaning.

ROD
Right.

AUTHOR
Did they say why they came to Earth? Was it planned or accidental?

MARINA
They were on a mission to seed this planet— as had other pods from their native planet—with beings of higher consciousness.

ROD
Their science and technology was light-years ahead of ours even now, and a scanner on their planet enabled them to analyze in detail very distant star systems in order to determine which were conducive to their kind of life.

AUTHOR
What did they look like back then?

MARINA
They walked upright on two legs and had a slight resemblance to human beings, although the brain cortex was more highly developed; hence there was a pronounced bulging of the skull from above the eyes to the top of the skull.

AUTHOR
So how did they become whales and dolphins?

ROD
Eventually, after living as land beings for a long time, they realized that the most superior quality of life could be had by living in the sea, where a plentiful supply of food was always available. In order to facilitate the biological transformations necessary to be able to live in the sea, genetic engineering was undertaken. Because family life was so important to this race of beings, and, therefore, the necessity of good communication, speech was modified and augmented by a kind of sonar, which in its extreme upper and lower ranges was able to pass through hundreds of miles of sea water, thereby becoming infinitely superior to the range of sound passing through air.

MARINA
Life in the sea proved to be idyllic, that is, until the nineteenth century, when the human race, whose ancestors existed only as tiny shrew-like creatures at the time of the coming of the pod, sought to harpoon the whales. Although that slaughter has largely abated, the dolphins tell us that more cetacean are dying now than ever before due to pollutants in the water which upset the delicate balance of their immune systems.

ROD
And one of the reasons for their desire to contact humans now, which is shared by *all* cetaceans they say, even killer whales, is to alert us to the fact that we are not only killing them but also our planet, and in so doing, killing ourselves.

MARINA
That is the evolutionary and environmental picture, but the metaphysical one that they present—with Ratava's help—is even more fascinating. To them all life possesses "soul," from the amoeba on upwards. From time to time, incarnations of the divine principle present throughout the universe appear in the

form of avatars. These avatars "speak" not only to humans, but to all the animals as well. Two of these avatars which dolphins have known as well as humans are Buddha and Jesus. When I told Darby and Joan that it was the words of Jesus which the school children were saying, Joan replied, "Jesus not say only humans have souls."

AUTHOR

I'm curious, does the cetacean collective consciousness have a mythology? I suppose they must if they are of a higher consciousness than our species, as they appear to be.

ROD

They also believe in a Second Coming, but their's is of the return of the Pod, the craft or ark that brought them here is given a deeply spiritual significance, and it will come to deliver them, or take then Above (Heaven in our terms) if they face annihilation from man's destruction of the planet, either through pollution or radioactivity due to warfare.

MARINA

The Second Coming of the Mother Pod will be anticipated by the incarnation of another avatar, who will be recognized by all cetaceans but not necessarily by Man. And the message he bears is not strict codes of conduct, as given by Avatars in the past, but to play, to *simply play*.

ROD

Because play duplicates the creative activity whereby the divine principle constantly recreates the universe.

MARINA

That "play" becomes more complex the higher the species in consciousness, and the highest activity that can be indulged in— in a spiritual sense— on Earth.

AUTHOR
"Follow your Bliss."

ROD
Joseph Campbell's message to the world.

AUTHOR
Yes. But what he meant by that is often misunderstood, because it is interpreted in the Western sense of narcissistic self-indulgence. The Bliss divine— that which Ramakrishna called *satchitananda*, Campbell said in *Philosophies of India*, is a state of mind in which one experiences sheer being (*sat*), consciousness (*cit*), and bliss (*ananda*) "as the transpersonal essence of his actual self."

MARINA
Ratava will be interested in talking to you.

AUTHOR
He knows Sanskrit, you said?"

MARINA
Yes, and many other languages. But doesn't seem to know much about literature. I've never seen him reading, other than the transcripts of the cetacean tapes.

ROD
I don't think he ever attended a university.

AUTHOR
That's probably to his credit.

MARINA
He should be back next week or the next.

AUTHOR
Well, I'll look forward to meeting him.

ROD
Now, I think we'd better head for home.

AUTHOR

Could I possibly stay and have a look at the transcripts?

ROD

We can leave you here, but you'll miss dinner.

AUTHOR

No problem, after that feast last night I can stand to miss a meal.

MARINA

Call us when you want a ride?

AUTHOR

Not necessary, I know the way and can walk back.

ROD

Well, don't forget that you can't get out of here once the door is locked. We have to lock it, but we'll prop the door open with a chair so that you can leave when you want to. You won't have any visitors. Once we drive out we'll tell the guard at the end of the road not to let anyone in. His number is on the wall if you have any problems.

MARINA

Goodnight, then.

AUTHOR

Goodnight.

INT. DOLPHIN CENTER - NIGHT
FULL SHOT - We are shooting from the lobby towards the illuminated doorway in the next room where the Author is sitting at a desk reading the transcripts of the whale "songs." Suddenly there is a rush of wind, a loud crash as the door which the Author had propped open slams shut. He gets up and tries the door, but it will not open.

> AUTHOR (Narr.)
> (returning to his desk)
> Rod and Marina warned me that I would be locked in if the door shut, and now it had happened. I started to call them to drive down and unlock the door to take me home, but one look at my watch told me they would be fast asleep. Fortunately there was a couch in the lobby and I decided to sleep there for the night. Because I knew that they would be ringing first thing in the morning when they realized I had not come home, I turned in at once.

CLOSE SHOT
The Author curling up on the couch.
SLOW DISSOLVE TO BLACK

SOUND OF DOLPHIN SQUEAKS GRADUALLY GROWING LOUDER, AS CAMERA CONTINUES ON BLACK.

> AUTHOR (Narr.)
> I had been asleep for what seemed a long time when I heard what I thought was Darby and Joan calling to me from their pool outside. I raised my head and listened, and then saw a tiny but very bright light passing like a laser over my head. I turned to look and realized that it was coming from the wall, as were the dolphin voices. At first I thought I must be dreaming, but knew at once that I was not. The light seemed to be coming from a small recessed tunnel in the wall. As I watched, I heard the dolphin voices coming from within the tunnel, but slowly moving nearer to me.
>
> Then I saw steps dimly illuminated in front of the tunnel, and a sea fan coral lit up like a Christmas tree in front of the tunnel, which I now saw was within a

pyramid crowned with a golden capstone. The light was streaming down the tunnel from an inner sanctum which must have been at the center of the pyramid. Outside the tunnel, as if guarding the entrance were two pillars.

Four dolphins hung nearly motionless just outside the doorway to the inner sanctum. Suddenly I realized that they were poised in the "X" shape of St. Andrew's cross, which designated the union of Upper and Lower Worlds. Immediately the cover illustration of *Tarot Revelations* flashed into my mind. But these were not *my* thoughts. It was the light that was sending me the information, almost in a telepathic way. I stopped trying to think, and relaxed my mind to become more receptive. Instantly a picture came into focus of the upper and lower trines on the toga of The Magus on the book cover. The "feminine" trine contained water drops falling down; the "masculine" trine enclosed fire and smoke ascending. In this one image all opposites were contained and resolved.

Then a new image of resolution entered my mind as swiftly as the last had come. The four dolphins were at the four points in the four directions, and as such signified the four elements, earth, air, water, and fire. This time I experienced a thrill, a shiver of harmony which seemed to resonate throughout the universe.

Within the pyramid, within the light, was a power source which was being beamed directly at me. But it was not mechanical in origin, but deeply personal. It was a Presence, gentle, careful to not overwhelm me with what it wished to convey, but powerful, the most powerful thing in the universe, I felt, and all-knowing. It knew my whole life as if I were but a microchip in its psychic circuitry, and it knew what I had been before the "me" that I was now, and what Earth had been before there had been Earth, and what Light had been when there was but Darkness in the universe.

And now it told me that it knew my future, and that

there was something I must do. There was a sudden surge, a powerful "message," a feeling of divine bliss, that flashed into my poor mind like a beacon and then out; out, out beyond me, beyond this world, in all directions at once, now already skirting the boundaries of our universe, seeding the eternal Darkness beyond with its loving Light.

It was gone. My mind came back to me. I looked again at the St. Andrew's cross made by the four dolphins' bodies. Words from Harold Bayley's *The Lost Language of Symbolism* now came to me, not from without, but from within my own memory banks. All the words for "cross", crux, cruz, krois, krouz have a common source in *-ak*, *-ur*, or *os*, revealing the spiritual fire symbolism in the "light of the Great Fire."

Yes, this was the way I thought, pulling up nearly unconscious contents as laboriously as a fisherman hauling in a net from a depth of ten thousand feet. But how much simpler life would be if we could all be enlightened as rapidly and as simply as I had been by the all-knowing Light.

My eyes focused again on the St. Andrews cross made by the four dolphins, the Upper and Lower Worlds wedded in the pattern of their bodies, and then I realized that a "wedding" had just occurred in my mind. I had been "seeded" by the Light of the Upper World. My poor gray cells constituted the Lower World to which the Light had descended as the One descends from Above to earth Below.

"St. Andrew," my mind said, and I pulled back slightly from the wall. For the first time I realized that I was looking at the painting on the wall of Andrew Annenberg.

Immediately with that realization the painting began to illuminate from within. There was still the white light in the pyramid's tunnel, but it was no longer the all-knowing Light which had flashed out into the universe. Sunlight now poured down from the surface of the ocean just over the roof of a temple, three marble columns of which still held it intact. A small pod of dolphins swam slowly past the temple roof, looking down towards the illuminated doorway of the pyramid, over which a humpbacked whale lazily undulated its flippers and began to sing. Sing! Swim! Yes, all the dolphins and the whale were now swimming! I could hear their liquid splashings.

Suddenly all the coral on the seafloor in the foreground flamed into color, along with wrasses, parrot fish, and a garibaldi. The coral bent to an invisible current, and the small fish swam in and out among the coral.

Crunch! Crunch! I could hear a parrot fish biting off a bit of coral.

The humpbacked whale swam out of the picture to the right, then reappeared in the distance behind the pyramid.

The dolphins had been gyrating in small circles around the temple pillars and around a statue of Winged Victory, a stand of coral protruding from where her head once had been.

Suddenly a crimson fish, cruising past a terra-cotta inlay of a boy riding the backs of two dolphins, blinked once at me, and then shot out of the painting past my head. He was out where the center of the lobby should have been, holding motionless and regarding me. I felt a surge pass my head and saw a solitary dolphin swim out, circle around, and pass back into the painting.

As if a cue to the other dolphins, they moved up to the edge of the painting, regarding me warily, and then forming a single pod they swam past me, all the time keeping their eyes upon me as if I were a keeper who would prevent their escape from the painting.

Once out, they now began to chase one another up and down in the lobby, cartwheeling and chirruping excitedly. Then I knew that they were talking to me, inviting me to play, but I did not know how to play.

The deep baying of the whale's song now became louder, as its bulk slowly loomed towards me. It paused a moment, as if waiting my permission, and then it too swam out. Instinctively, I ducked my head.

Slowly circling in the lobby, and all the time regarding me with one eye as they passed, the dolphins and the whale now began a cetacean chorus that seemed directed at me.

If I could not play, could I at least get their message? They were natural telepaths. All I had to do was relax and receive, as I had done for the White Light.

Then the message came clearly. It was the same as "play," follow your heart of bliss, my mentor's message also. It was coming from all sides, from every cetacean brain in the lobby, and from beyond, from every cetacean in the sea. They wanted to tell me something else, something beyond bliss, more dire, of great significance to the race of Man, and to Earth, Mother of all living things. I could not get the content of their message, but I got its feeling. It was desperate and full of warning.

Then the distant cetacean voices grew fainter, ceased, and the swimmers in the lobby, with one last earnest look, passed by me into the painting. The illumination from within faded and went out. I was alone again in the silent darkness.

Eventually I slept.

SLOW DISSOLVE

SOUND OF RINGING PHONE BEFORE FADE-IN
MED SHOT - Author sleeping on couch. He gets up and walks to next
room to answer phone.

> AUTHOR
> Oh, hello, Marina.
> (listening)
> No, I succeeded in locking myself in, and it was too
> late to call. I slept on the couch.
> (listening again)
> Well, if Rod's on his way, then I'll see you later.

As soon as he puts down the phone, SOUND OF FRONT DOOR
OPENING CAN BE HEARD FROM LOBBY.

FULL SHOT
Rod opens the door and looks down the length of the lobby. The floor
is covered with water. As he is standing there looking at it, the Author
enters the lobby from the other end. He pauses, looking where Rod
is gazing.

> ROD
> Where did all this water come from? Did a pipe burst
> last night?

> AUTHOR
> (kneeling down and tasting
> the water)
> Salt water.

> ROD
> (half annoyed)
> The tide can't get in here. What the hell happened?!

> AUTHOR
> I don't really know. But the picture came to life, and
> they were all swimming out here in the lobby.

> ROD
> Do you take drugs, man?! Is that why you wanted to
> stay here alone last night?!

                    AUTHOR
No, I've never taken drugs in my life.

                      ROD
Well, you were here! Didn't you notice the water
before?!

                    AUTHOR
I just woke up. I didn't get much sleep last night.

                      ROD
                 (exasperated)
Okay, if that's all you want to tell me.

                    AUTHOR
I want to go in a room— alone— and write down what
happened so that I can remember every detail.

                      ROD
Meanwhile I'll get out the mop and clean it up. Marina
is bringing down breakfast. I walked down.

                    AUTHOR
              (walking towards door)
See you soon.

CUT TO FULL SHOT
Rod has propped open the lobby door to facilitate the floor's drying.
Marina enters and engages in conversation with Rod, expressing
disbelief at what he says. Then with an impatient gesture he
indicates the painting and shakes his head. Marina steps closer to
the painting.

                    MARINA
                  (gasping)
Oh, my god! He shouldn't have!

                      ROD
                (going to her side)
What?!

MARINA
(pointing)
He's ruined the painting!

SLOW DOLLY IN to center of the Annenberg painting where on top of a marble pedestal, leaning against the sea fan coral, is the book *Tarot Revelations*, with the author's name plainly visible.

MARINA
(angrily)
Where is he?

CLOSE UP

AUTHOR
Right here.

MED SHOT

AUTHOR
(continuing)
Perhaps you'd better read this. I'm going swimming with Darby and Joan.

He hands her the account he has just written of his experience with the painting the previous night.

FADE OUT

INT. ROD AND MARINA'S HOUSE - DAY
The living room and kitchen are really one room divided by a counter running half the length of the room. One week later.

MED SHOT

MARINA
Are you ready for some more synchronicities, Richard?

AUTHOR
Shoot.

MARINA

You remember I told you we were going to dinner at the home of some friends of ours

AUTHOR

Yes.

MARINA

Well, Andrew Annenberg and his business manager Ardath are going to be there.

AUTHOR

Incredible.

ROD

And we have not said a word to anyone about your experience with the painting. But if you want to tell Andrew about it, I think it might be a good idea to have him come over here tonight after the dinner to inspect the painting.

AUTHOR

For what reason?

ROD

To verify that the painting has not been tampered with. It is a cibrachrome film copy of the original. There are fifty of these cibrachrome copies in the series, about half of which have been sold to date.

AUTHOR

What an ingenious idea. That way fifty more people can share in the experience of the painting rather than one.

MARINA

I think it was Ardath's idea. Andrew is sort of a dreamer and visionary, but Ardath is very practical.

AUTHOR

They sound like a good combination.

ROD

Anyhow, I believe Andrew or Ardath— or both— supervised the framing of the Dolphin Center's cibrachrome because it was one of the first ones in the series. The glass cannot touch the film, so it is a tricky business.

MARINA

Oh, I see what you're driving at, Rod, if the glass had been removed or the frame tampered with, then Andrew or Ardath would know it by inspecting the painting.

AUTHOR

You still don't believe me.

ROD

Yes, we do believe you, but unless we can tell the director of the Center that Andrew inspected it, he is certainly not going to believe us.

MARINA

And another thing comes to mind, Richard, if your book is there in the painting on film, and it of course is not in the original; then instead of decreasing the value it may enhance it many times.

ROD

By god, you're right, Marina. We could have *millions* of people paying an admission just to see the painting, and maybe stay around to learn something about dolphins. Richard, you may have saved the Dolphin Center.

AUTHOR

But I still say I didn't *do* anything.

MARINA

Maybe not, but you were the catalyst for whatever happened.

INT. THE HOME OF PHIL AND LOUISE WINSTON - NIGHT
The house has a large bay window which commands an extraordinary view of the sunset now taking place.

MONTAGE of shots of arrival at house, introduction of the Author to the hosts, pouring of drinks, and eating of snacks.

> AUTHOR (Narr.)
> I was to meet Andrew Annenberg at the home of Phillip and Louise Winston. Circumstances had permitted Phil to retire at the age of 45, and now at 50 he was enjoying the oceanic ambience of life on Maui. His principle interest in life now seemed to be in championing the cause of saving our cetacean friends, and in so doing he and his wife devoted many hours to fund-raising for the Atlantis Dolphin Center. When I arrived, Andrew and Ardath had not yet made their appearance, but I was only shortly disappointed.

FULL SHOT of front door and SOUND OF DOORBELL. Louise opens door, ZOOM IN on Andrew and Ardath.

> AUTHOR (Narr.)
> Andrew Annenberg was a tall, gangling man. He took in the room with an all-encompassing, penetrating gaze that seemed to suggest to me that he already knew everything about me, even though we had never met.

> His companion, Ardath, a striking brunette, was nearly as tall, but whereas Andrew's spirit seemed not completely at home in its captive body, Ardath reminded one of a willow tree, as she moved with easy grace across the room towards me.

> ARDATH
> (extending her hand)
> I'm Ardath, Richard. Marina has loaned me *From Eden to Eros*, and I want you to know that if there were more men in the world like you, we wouldn't have a war of the sexes.

AUTHOR
Thank you, I was beginning to wonder if anyone was reading the book.

Annenberg is still near the front door, where he is being introduced to Rod and Marina by the Winstons.

ARDATH
(taking the Author's hand)
Come and meet Andrew.
(walking up to Annenberg)
Andrew, this is Richard Roberts.

ANDREW
Oh, pleased to meet you.

AUTHOR
And I you. "Aqueous Atlantis" has proved to be an experience in more ways than one.

ANDREW
(looking somewhat puzzled)
Oh?

MARINA
We'll tell you more of that over dinner.

ROD
Could you stop down at the Atlantis Dolphin Center with us on your way home?

ANDREW
I already had a swim with dolphins today.

MARINA
That's not the reason. We have something incredible to show you.

MED SHOT - SLOW PAN around the dinner table.

AUTHOR (Narr.)
Annenberg had begun drawing from the time his

parents took him on a visit to the Smithsonian Institute in Washington at the age of seven. His vision of nature and his unabashed enthusiasm seemed to come from being deeply in touch with the Wonder Child within. Listening to him, I was reminded of some lines by Chuang Tsu. "It is the child that sees the secret in Nature, and it is the child of ourselves we return to. The child within us is simple and daring enough to live the Secret."

Somehow Annenberg was in touch with a secret that had enabled his canvas to come alive in my presence. Suddenly a dream which I had not thought of in many years flashed into my head. I was in a bookstore which had round cushions centered around a pole which reached to the ceiling. The bookshelves also extended to the ceiling. Because I was tall, by standing on my tip-toes I was able to reach a book, which upon being opened revealed natural scenes in which clouds moved across the page and out of sight at the book's margin, and the trees swayed to an invisible breeze. "What wondrous book is this?" I thought, treating it with awe. But next to me a baby had been sat, who grasped at the book and began removing its pages, replacing them in a different order. Later a psychic friend interpreted the dream for me.

"The Book of the Secret of Nature is being opened for you, but it is of a different order or reality than you apprehend. Listen to the child within."

CLOSE UP - Andrew Annenberg

ANDREW
(to the Author seated at his
side)
Your child redeems his own parents.

CUT BETWEEN AUTHOR AND ANNENBERG

AUTHOR
What?

64

ANDREW
Bertie, your hero in *The Wind and the Wizard* is an orphan.

AUTHOR
Yes.

ANDREW
Like the abandoned child motif of mythology. And like the myth of the Divine Child, Bertie is a child of Light.

AUTHOR
How so?

ANDREW
Because as a physicist when he grows up he will bring to the world new models of space/time in which Light— with a capital "L" as you say— is factored into the equation.

AUTHOR
Yes, in that sense he *is* the mythic Child of Light.

ANDREW
And like the Avatars of history, he brings Light and a new order.

AUTHOR
Yes, of course!
(musing for a moment) Well, I hope I can one day supply you with an artistic critique of one of your paintings equal to what you have just given me.

MED SHOT

ROD
(tapping on glass with spoon)
Attention, ladies and gentlemen. Court is now in session. I have just one question for the witness, Andrew Annenberg. Did you or did you not know about Richard's book *Tarot Revelations* when you were painting "Aqueous Atlantis"?

                    ANDREW
                (looking surprised)
Uh, no, I did not. Someone gave it to me only last
month...Why?
                    ROD
                (to Marina)
There! You see!

                    MARINA
We have a story to tell about the "Aqueous Atlantis"
in the lobby of the Dolphin Center.

                    ANDREW
And Ardath has a story about "The Portal of Hunab
Ku."

                    AUTHOR
What is that?

                    ARDATH
It's another of Andrew's paintings. It's somewhat like
"Aqueous Atlantis," but there is an underwater Mayan
temple in this one. But mine is a long story, and I
think we'd better save it until after dinner, or I won't
be able to get a bite to eat, and I see Louise has
prepared her usual extraordinary gourmet dinner.

Everyone compliments Louise.

                    ARDATH
What I want to ask you, Richard, is how you ever got
the idea that Eve, serpent, and the Tree of Genesis
actually stood for a constellation worshipped by the
followers of the Mother Goddess. I mean, millions,
even billions of people had read the Bible and everyone just accepted this talking snake and a woman
willing to listen to him.

                    LOUISE
Ardath, there are a lot of talking snakes, unfortunately, these days that women listen to.

AUTHOR

Well, Joseph Campbell always said, "You can't read the Bible as history," although some still insist on doing so. Anyhow, basically when one thinks "tree" in a mythological sense, one thinks of the World/Axis/Tree, or the Tree of Life, which appears in the B.C. mythologies of the Middle East. Therefore, the Eden tree has an implied vertical axis which extends to a cosmic source whereby the world is renewed.

ARDATH

So it was just by logical reasoning that you arrived at the answer? If that's so, I would have thought that any mythologist would have discovered it.

AUTHOR

You're right, it did require more than logic; it required a trip to Paradise.

ARDATH

Paradise?!

PHIL

Sounds like a shamanistic flight to heaven. Do you know the story of Wovoka, the Paiute shaman?

AUTHOR

No.

ROD

We neglected to tell you, Richard, that Phil is particularly interested in the mythologies of the American Indian, and quite a fan of Joseph Campbell's.

AUTHOR

Well, I can tell you some personal stories about Joe, regarding the Indians, that I'm sure you'd find interesting, but go on with your story.

PHIL

This is reported in volume one of Campbell's *Historical Atlas of World Mythology* subtitled The *Way of the*

Animal Powers. At the time— 1889— of an eclipse of the sun (which as you know was fraught with dread for the Indian because the sun was the life principle) the shaman Wovoka had a vision which was to revolutionize the mythology of the remaining plains Indians. He said, "I went up to heaven and saw God and all the people who had died a long time ago. God told me to come back and tell my people they must be good and love one another, and not fight or steal, or lie. He gave me this dance to give my people."

Now you have to realize what a radical thing it was to tell Indians not to fight one another, but to love, because the warrior was the very essence of their culture.

ANDREW
What was the dance God gave him?

LOUISE
The Charleston.

Laughter from around the table.

PHIL
The Ghost Dance, so named because it anticipated an immediate regeneration of the earth, the end of the White Man, and the *resurrection* of all dead Indians from the beginning of the earth, and also the return from the dead of the buffalo herds.

ANDREW
Powerful stuff.

PHIL
Yes, it swept across the Plains like wildfire. All these tribes that had been killing one another for centuries suddenly joined hands and danced in a circle, thanks to the vision of one man, Wovoka. But you were telling the story of *your* trip to Paradise, Richard.

AUTHOR

Well, *my* Paradise is an island in the Bahamas, and the place of my divine inspiration from the Goddess— not God—was "Open-Circuit Bridge."

PHIL

I guess in Paradise *all* the circuits are open.

AUTHOR

I was on vacation there with my brother and sister. There is another little island just off shore, and I had bribed somebody to take me there so that I could swim back to Paradise Island. I got out of the boat about twenty yards from the little island and thought I would do some snorkeling before swimming back. I put on my mask and went under and saw that my side of the island was entirely ringed by barracuda, not in a school formation, but side by side like pickets in a fence—and they were big. Usually barracuda won't attack a swimmer unless you have something shiny, but it occurred to me that if one went after me the others probably would too; so without making any waves I backed out of there as carefully as possible. I started swimming back, heading for the "Open-Circuit-Bridge", where I had hitched a ride. I had on swim fins, but the first thing I noticed was that there was a terrific current, and I had to swim at a forty-five degree angle. This meant that the length of the swim would now be doubled. Still it seemed okay. But the closer I got to shore, the more I was carried north-ward, away from the shore. Eventually, I was hoping to make landfall at the tip of a spit of land about a mile north of where I started. If I missed that, there was nothing but open ocean all the way to New York. My brother and sister were walking along the shoreline keeping pace, but they thought I was swimming parallel to the beach for exercise!

ARDATH

Well, you're here, so I guess you didn't drown.

AUTHOR

No, but I just made it in. There is a little bridge over a canal to a lagoon on the island. Timothy Wyllie, who wrote *Dolphins Extraterrestrials Angels* tells about standing on the bridge at precisely midnight of the Vernal equinox, 1982, when three waves roared up the canal into the lagoon where several dolphins were held for show performances. He recalls shouting, "The circuits are opening!" He says that the dolphins and the entities that guided them were involved with sustaining the more subtle energies at work on the planet— for its preservation, I guess— and that the waves conducted information essential to the captive dolphins. You'd have to see the canal and the bridge to appreciate the unlikelihood of those three waves making it in from the ocean.

Anyhow, my experience on the bridge occurred before his and before reading his book. It happened the night of the day of the long swim I had, and I was feeling very lucky to be alive, looking up at the stars in appreciative wonder. In order to get my bearings in the sky, I started looking for the Pole Star, Polaris. My thought was, "It's at the top of the tree," and I felt I was standing at the center of this World/Axis/Tree and *my* spine was incorporated into it. I found Polaris and a few other constellations, and then when I saw Draco I began to wonder if any of Draco's stars were ever the pole star, which would have put it in the Tree. The body of the Mother Goddess was also thought of as a life-giving Tree. All of a sudden, I felt that this constellation and the Tree were the Eve, serpent, and tree of the bible. Later scholarship set me back momentarily when I found that Draco was not a serpent but a dragon, but eventually I learned that it was a serpent even earlier. Thuban in Draco was the pole star in 6,000 B.C., the era of the Goddess, and Eltanin, one of its stars, was associated in the minds of worshippers with the Goddess. All of Joseph Campbell's material on the serpent as consort of the Goddess clinched it for me. Oh, and the big moment came when one of the astronomers at the planetarium in San Francisco regressed the sky for me to show what it looked like in 6,000 B.C. with the serpent in the tree.

PHIL

Obviously then, this was a celestial configuration that inspired awe and reverence in the minds of the people at that time. In Genesis it becomes the greatest of all evils, and Eve is blamed for the Fall of Man.

AUTHOR

Precisely, that is why I subtitled *From Eden to Eros, Origins of the Put Down of Women*. The writer or writers of the book of Genesis are attempting to denigrate the Great Mother Goddess of the earlier religion in order to supplant that religion with their own. But the Old Testament is not a religious document but a political ax-grinding, a social document of do's and don't's, or thou shalt nots. Joseph Campbell told me that he once gave it to a Hindu to read, and he returned the bible with the comment, "I can't find any religion in it".

MARINA

But look how it controlled everyone's lives from then until now.

AUTHOR

Yes, unfortunately. Half of the population— women— were treated as economic slaves, and their potential denied them for two thousand years. And instead of living in harmony with our bodies and with nature, we sought to tame and conquer nature, and that has inevitably led to the present ecological mess and an entire culture that is or should be on a psychoanalyst's couch. There, I've got that off my chest, and as Joseph Campbell would say, "Who needs Abraham's bosom?!"

Laughter around the table.

PHIL

Well, I can see why Marina thought you could be of

71

help to the Dolphin Center. Obviously "saving the dolphins" is part of a larger picture in your mind, a kind of "psychic ghost dancing" in which you might hope to resurrect the harmony of a time when the race was a caretaker of earth and its creatures. You would have made a good Indian, Richard.

> AUTHOR
> I've never been ashamed of being who I am until I saw "Dances with Wolves," and then I wanted to slink out the back door. We wiped that profoundly spiritual culture off the face of North America, and replaced it with a facetious society of bible-thumpers seeking ultimately to conquer nature in the same way that they had conquered the Indian and tamed women collectively. Of course, they tried to kill all the whales, and I'm here now to draw a line and say to them, "If you want to kill the whales and dolphins, you'll have to kill me first. And that goes for Mother Earth, too, Gaia. No more pollution, no more rainforests cut down!"
>> (looking down at his plate)
> I've forgotten my dinner.

CUT TO MED SHOT
Later that same evening. Plates have been cleared, and coffee or brandy is served.

> AUTHOR
> I have a little surprise. Some of the whale transcripts have yielded results.

> MARINA
> Why didn't you tell us before?

> AUTHOR
> Because it required the proper setting and the right audience. We have it here. Seven people who care very deeply about saving cetaceans; yet I'm sure no one would argue that we have the right to kill them if we choose to do so.

72

ARDATH
What are you talking about, Richard?!

ROD
He's kidding, he's got to be kidding.

LOUISE
I'm not sure he is.

AUTHOR
I was merely citing the validation of the bible, since we are given dominion over the fowl in the skies, the fish in the sea.

MARINA
Oh, I see what you're driving at.

AUTHOR
Well, wait till you hear this transcript from Greek of a whale song. Incidentally, Phil, I've learned that you are the one responsible for supplying the funds for the ships and hydrophones to record all of these songs. I think when you learn the source of this one, you'll feel rewarded for your efforts and astounded. The telepathic meaning, as rendered by Ratava is as follows:

> "The thoughtless tribe of birds,
>   The beasts that roam the fields
>   The brood in sea-depths born,
>   He takes them all in nets,
>   Knotted in snaring mesh,
>   Man, wonderful in skill."

MARINA
It sounds like the whale is praising us for capturing the world's creatures.

ROD
Why would a whale be singing that?!

                    ANDREW
Doesn't make sense.

                    AUTHOR
Now get ready for a shock. The whale is "singing" the
words of a man.

                    PHIL
What?!

                    ROD
How can that be?

                    AUTHOR
Sophocles. Antistrope I from *Antigone*.

A babble of voices ensues.

                    AUTHOR (Narr.)
I didn't blame them for being so excited. I was too
when I identified the passage. We were quite a team.
Phil had the money to give us the technology necessary to retrieve the "songs" from the oceans' depths.
Ratava had the telepathic ability to receive the meaning of the whale song, and my earlier background as
a professor of literature enabled me to identify the
human source of that song.

                    PHIL
I'm somewhat unclear on what Ratava is doing with
the transcripts. He didn't write out the interpretation
of the whale song in the Greek of Sophocles' day did
he?

                    AUTHOR
From what I have been able to gather from the tapes,
they are what we would rightly call a song and not
attempts at human speech, such as the dolphin-say
that Marina and Rod have taught to Darby and Joan.

PHIL

Then how does Ratava convert the whale-song into English?

AUTHOR

Telepathically. The whale "means" something as he sings. Ratava picks up the meaning instantaneously, because there is no distance in telepathic communication. This has wider implications in that the dolphins and whales may now be sending telepathic messages back to their native planet.

MARINA

What kind of a message might they be sending?

AUTHOR

"Help! Help! This planet is polluted and dying."

PHIL

Do any of the transcripts of whale song contain such a message?

AUTHOR

No, and they probably would not, because you see the whale song utilizes water as the medium for its transmission.

ANDREW

So whale-song is only for the ears of other whales.

ROD

Right.

PHIL

Well, then if Ratava listens to a tape of whale song after its transmission, how can he get the meaning, since that comes only while the song is being sung.

AUTHOR

He can't. You've hit on something very important, which I noticed only after realizing that his transcriptions cover only those tapes which he is listening to as they are being sent. Thus Ratava must be present or we'll never get a meaning.

PHIL
Why didn't somebody realize that earlier? I have ships at sea now making tapes, and I understand he is in India.

ROD
Well, it may be possible sometime in the future to develop a kind or Rosetta Stone which will enable us to decipher the other tapes by extrapolating from the deciphered songs Ratava has made.

PHIL
Yes, I suppose that is a possibility, but I think money is better spent on recording a whale-song *only* when Ratava is available to listen.

LOUISE
I think Phillip is right.

ARDATH
Andrew and I have never met Ratava. Is there a chance that he will be back soon?

MARINA
He comes and goes rather mysteriously.

ARDATH
How many tapes do you have for which Ratava has supplied a telepathic interpretation?

MARINA
One, maybe, two hundred, wouldn't you say, Rod?

ROD
Yes.

AUTHOR
I think they should be published, because the more persons who see the transcripts, the more likely they

are to be identified.

PHIL
Why do you say "identified"? Are you implying that they all are excerpts from literature?

LOUISE
That seems absurd.

AUTHOR
Well, listen to this next one. It is in both Latin and English, as Ratava has transcribed it. "On account of their warm bilocular heart, their lungs, their moveable eyelids, their hollow ears, *penem intrantem, feminiam mammis lactantem,* and finally *ex lege naturae jure meritoque.*"

MARINA
That's it?

AUTHOR
That's it. Any takers?

Everyone looks very puzzled. After a moment, Phil speaks.

PHIL
It seems crazy, but I'm sure I've heard that before.

ANDREW
If we could figure out to whom *their* heart, *their* lungs, *their* ears refers, we could probably decipher it.

ROD
Since the whale in Sophocles' song was singing about mankind, could this be the same thing?

AUTHOR
Well, no, because the Latin refers to the biological characteristics of whales, that is why they are considered mammals. It is the way in which a natural history book would classify them scientifically.

ROD
So the point of view here is that of man.

AUTHOR
Precisely.

MARINA
(chuckling)
That makes it even more curious. A whale describing its own biology from the point of view of man.

AUTHOR
Well, if you all give up, I can tell you that the words are from Linnaeus' eighteenth century natural history *System of Nature*. He is citing the anatomical reasons why he classifies whales as mammals rather than fishes.

PHIL
This is very strange. I know I've never read Linnaeus, but I know that passage from another source, I just can't put my finger on it.

ROD
So the whale is citing the reason why man classifies his species as mammals not fishes?

AUTHOR
Evidently.

MARINA
God, this gets weirder and weirder.

While they are talking, Phil goes into an adjacent room, his library, takes down a book, and begins riffling through it. Presently he returns to the dining room with the book in hand.

PHIL
Moby Dick.

LOUISE
No?!

ANDREW

Can you believe it!

MARINA

Amazing!

PHIL

Chapter thirty-two, "Cetology." *"Their"* heart, lungs, and ears refers to the whales' anatomy. I guess Melville is citing Linnaeus' reasons for classifying whales as mammals.

ROD

But why would they be reciting man's definition of them?

AUTHOR

Don't ask me. What happened with Andrew's painting blew all my circuits. Nothing would surprise me now.

ANDREW

I want to hear about that.

AUTHOR

And I want to hear Ardath's account of what happened with her and the other painting. Have you written it down?
(to Ardath)

ARDATH

No, it only happened last week.

AUTHOR

About 2:00 a.m. last Tuesday night?

ARDATH

(to Andrew)
How many hours ahead of Hawaii time is it in the Yucatan?

ANDREW
Three or four hours I guess.

ARDATH
That would be the time and date then.

MARINA
More synchronicities.

LOUISE
Before she gets started, would anyone like more coffee or another drink?

Various requests are given and fulfilled by Louise, assisted by Marina. When everyone has settled down again, Ardath begins her story.

ARDATH
I won't go into all the details of what led up to my being in the Yucatan, other than to say that three days earlier I had participated in a Balche ceremony with Lacandon Indians. Balche is a fermented liquor made from the tree's bark and shared in the village Godhouse with the shaman. After drinking the Balche, I felt relaxed and acutely perceptive, but not "stoned." Subsequently I began to get the feeling that I must call Andrew, but that was not possible because we were far from a phone. Three nights later this dream occurred.

CLOSE SHOT of Ardath, eyes closed. Slowly she opens them.

MED SHOT. A luxurious room in a Japanese hotel, indicated by the decor. A KNOCK AT THE DOOR SOUNDS.
Ardath puts on a kimono, then calls for the person to enter. A Japanese girl enters with a tray of tea and rice cakes. Bowing she sets it on the table before Ardath.

ARDATH (Narr.)
Andrew and I had come to Japan to oversee the installation of "Aqueous Atlantis" and "Portal of Hunab Ku" in a unique marine museum. The paintings had

80

been sold just before I had left for the Yucatan.

Ardath has drunk her tea and dressed when there is a SOUND OF KNOCKING ON DOOR. She opens the door. Two smiling Japanese men bow to her, SPEAKING JAPANESE, which is not subtitled. They escort her down the hall, which turns into another hall, all the time CHATTERING JAPANESE AS LIGHTING BECOMES DIMMER AND THEY MOVE IN PROGRESSIVELY SLOWER MOTION. THE SPOKEN JAPANESE GRADUALLY BLENDS INTO THE CHATTER OF DOL-PHINS. DOLLY IN RAPIDLY TO CLOSE SHOT of a doorway, on which is inscribed the words "ORACLE OF DELPHYS." MED SHOT

SHOOTING FROM BEHIND ARDATH'S HEAD AT THE DOOR. CHAT-TERING OF DOLPHINS GROWS LOUDER. She turns around to her Japanese escorts, and they have become dolphins, or rather, heads of dolphins with the bodies of the same Japanese men. The door opens on its own; they enter. Ahead lies a plush recliner chair, lying in one half of a transparent plastic bubble. The upper half is hinged like a clamshell. Ardath enters and reclines on the chair, whereupon the two dolphin-men lower the upper dome, which snaps in place. CAMERA SUDDENLY BLACK. SIMULTANEOUS WITH STEPHEN KINDLER MUSIC, FAINT LIGHT BEGINS as vertical columns of beams, illuminating the Annenberg painting "Portal of Hunab Ku." SOUND OF WHALE SONG AND DOLPHINS. At left in the painting is a Mayan temple, from which a bright light radiates. The temple has been engulfed by water, and fish, dolphins, whales, and a giant turtle swim around the ruins. ALL IMAGERY WITHIN PAINTING IS THREE-DIMENSIONAL, which is attained by holographic imaging of the scene's components. The first "movement" within the painting begins with the giant turtle, its head turning to regard the viewer, the point of view for which is Ardath's. Then very slowly, the turtle undulates its flippers and begins moving toward the viewer. About half-way to the viewer, the turtle begins to swim upwards, passing so close overhead that the individual plates in its soft underbody are clearly delineated. During this, the whales and dolphins have also "come to life." Gradually, many of the dolphins also swim out of the painting, and their chatter may be heard behind the viewer. Fish swim to and fro and coral sways to an invisible current. Finally, all the creatures that have left the painting return to their original positions, becoming motionless, as LIGHTS AND MUSIC FADE.

FADE OUT

INT. HOME OF PHIL AND LOUISE WINSTON - NIGHT
When Ardath had finished her story, a hush fell over the room. The similarities to my experience were astounding. Rod and Marina had not told anyone of my adventure with "Aqueous Atlantis" so Ardath had no clues to go by, but it was obvious that she had not made-up the story. Annenberg's paintings had become the focal point of this synchronistic phenomena, and the unanswered question was why. Although Annenberg had painted two incredibly visionary pictures, he did not appear to be a shaman or a magician on the order of Aleister Crowley. Then it hit me! The whales and dolphins were creating the phenomena, using their highly developed neo-cortex to communicate in startling ways. They had my attention for sure. But what was the purpose behind it?

Louise has again freshened the drinks and filled the coffee cups of the guests.

LOUISE
(pouring a beer for the
Author)
You should see Phil's library, Richard.

PHIL
Yes, let me show it to you. It's larger than all the public libraries on the island combined.

AUTHOR
I should be coming here instead of to the library.

PHIL
Feel free to do so. If I'm not home, one of the staff can let you in. Come, I'll show you.

As the Author joins Phil in the next room, Andrew and Ardath follow.

ARDATH
Do we get to hear your story?

AUTHOR
Oh, yes.

PHIL
I just wanted Richard to see my collection of Joseph

82

Campbell's books.
(indicating nearly an entire
shelf)

ANDREW
I'm a Joseph Campbell fan too.

PHIL
Who isn't these days? Without the Moyer's inter-
views, TV would be a wasteland.

AUTHOR
I see one of his books you don't have.

PHIL
Oh? I thought I had every one.

AUTHOR
No, *Where the Two Came to Their Father* was the first
book in the Bollingen Foundation series. And when
you consider that the complete works of Jung...

PHIL
(indicating the next shelf)
Here.

AUTHOR
...are in the series, it was quite an honor that Joseph
Campbell was involved in the project that produced
the first book.

PHIL
Well, tell me about it.

AUTHOR
Henrich Zimmer's suggestion was that the first book
in the Bollingen series should be a product not of the
East, or of the old European tradition of the West, but
of native America, and so he chose a Navaho War
Ceremonial which was given to Joe and Maud Oakes,
an artist, by Jeff King, an old medicine man of the
Navajo tribe. It was 1943, and the all but forgotten
rites of this ceremony were being revived on the

reservation to bless the young braves being inducted into the armed services.

                    ARDATH
How appropriate.

                    AUTHOR
The principal hero of *Where the Two Came to Their Father* is a god known to the Jicarilla Apache of the southwest. Before the moment of his last departure from his people he says, "The earth, the sky, the water is my body, and the seasons too. But don't think that I am just in the east, south, west, or north, or under the earth, or up in the sky, I am everywhere." And he tells them, "I have given you the two kinds of pipes for making an offering to me."

Joe wrote the accompanying commentary on this rite of passage. He notes that this Apache god is of the order of the incarnating Avatars even though we cannot say that he ever lived historically, as did Jesus and the Buddha. But his name, Monster-Slayer, reveals that he has a certain cosmic significance as a slayer of darkness in the never ending battle between light and darkness.

But the extraordinary thing about this book is that it is accompanied by 18 plates of the pollen paintings made by the medicine man and reproduced by the painter Maud Oakes.

The first time that I drove Joseph Campbell to Esalen in Big Sur, California, we had a beautiful luncheon with Maud up at her house on Partington Ridge, Big Sur. Then she moved to a condo in the Carmel Valley, and on another occasion we stayed overnight there on our way to Esalen. I think she was about seventy years old then— the late 1960's— but she was an incredibly beautiful woman, both outwardly and in spirit. One could see why a shaman would want to pass on sacred pollen paintings to her.

84

ARDATH
What is a pollen painting?

AUTHOR
The paintings are made with the pollen of flowers, plants, and trees, ground-up flowers, and cornmeal on a buckskin, with the head of the animal facing east, which is the quarter of the rising sun, the direction of new life, and there is a color associated with each quarter.

Phil takes down from his shelves, Campbell's *The Way of the Animal Powers* and opens it to "The Emergence," a Navaho sand paintings.

PHIL
(to Richard)
Probably you know this Navaho sand painting. "The Emergence." It's associated with the Upward-Reaching Rite. The people first emerge from the earth using a ladder made from four rays of the sun, each of a different color, pulled down to each one of the four quarters of the earth. Here you see the Emergence Ladder at the center and the ascending peoples' footprints starting from the white east and emerging at the yellow west. Four tribes or peoples of the myth wear the colors of the four directions.

ANDREW
It's like a Tibetan mandala, isn't it? The four quarters and a spiritual center resolving all the oppositions.

PHIL
Precisely.

ANDREW
(to Phil)
You don't have the book Joseph Campbell wrote with Richard on the Tarot symbology.

ARDATH
But it's more than that.
(to Richard)

As you say, the Tarot is a Western Book of the Dead.

                    AUTHOR
        (to Phil)
I'll bring you a copy and autograph it the next time I
come over.

                    PHIL
Oh, that will be nice. What was it like collaborating
with Joseph Campbell?

                    AUTHOR
Like participating in The Great Work.

                    PHIL
Of alchemy?

                    AUTHOR
Yes. But before we started our collaboration, I had a
Jungian Big Dream, as they say, about The Great
Work.

                    ARDATH
I love to hear people tell their dreams.

                    ANDREW
Tell it.

                    AUTHOR
This occurred in the early 1970's probably. Three or
four times a year Joe would be in the San Francisco
Bay Area to give seminars, and I would drive him to
these, and he would stay at my house in between the
seminars, often for nearly a week. So we started doing
some seminars together on Jung and Joyce, among
others. Often there was a kind of classroom setting,
such as the University of California Medical Center.
In the dream I am in a classroom with Joe and
another man, and we are actually involved in the
Great Work. We had to tutor a young boy in order to
make ends meet, and he was such a discipline
problem, preventing us from doing our work, that we

warned his grandmother that we would kick him out of the classroom.

Now in Jungian terms, you have to remember that the elements of the dream are all aspects of the dreamer; therefore, the kid who is the discipline problem represents my inferior function-sensation of the four Jungian functions: intuition, thinking, and feeling being the other three. To kick the kid out of the classroom would mean out of consciousness. The anima, the feminine archetype in the unconscious mind, often personifies the unconscious function.

ARDATH
You call the anima "Miss Right" in From *Eden to Eros*.

AUTHOR
Yes, in her positive aspect she represents all that a man desires to complete or fulfill within himself. We meet her in the world, however, in her negative aspect when we have neglected our own inner feminine and instead seek her in the outer world. The alchemical texts say that the "wife" of the alchemist has to be involved in the Great Work, meaning it can be attained only by the cooperation of the conscious and unconscious minds.

PHIL
Well, Jung thought alchemy was never really just a chemical science, but really a subtle psychology.

AUTHOR
Yes, I think you're right. Anyhow, you see how the conscious work we are doing in the classroom becomes too one-sided when we— or I— want to kick out the unconscious function, personified by the unruly boy. But the negative anima warns us that she will drive us out of the classroom, that is, out of our *minds*, if the boy goes. And what she does is to apport out of thin air writhing masses of snakes. Obviously we vacate the classroom fast. Then she gives me her terms for letting us back in so that we can go on with the Great Work.

First, I have to eat a nut from a small tree she tends, knowing full well that it may be poison and the end of my life. I undertake the sacrifice and become as if dead, asleep or lifeless, but in the end I revive.

The interesting thing is that fifteen years later when I wrote *The Wind and the Wizard*, I used a structure of six books, each representing a different element—as in alchemy—and seen as two interpenetrating trines, which is a symbol of the philosopher's stone, or the Great Work. And, of course, my boy protagonist undertakes the Great Work with the help of the Wizard of Oz.

ANDREW
But that's not the most important thing about the relation between *The Wind and the Wizard* and the Great Work.

AUTHOR
It's not?

ANDREW
No. Remember you told how you wrote it. A blend of conscious and unconscious minds.

AUTHOR
Yes, of course! I'd almost forgotten that the book was mostly a right brain product and a channeling from the unconscious anima.

PHIL
That's a good example of the way in which the conscious mind wants to take credit for everything.

ARDATH
And why in the dream you had to sacrifice consciousness so that the Great Work could be completed.

PHIL
And I guess the ego had to be sacrificed also, because at first in the dream you were in charge of the classroom, and then grandmother anima showed you who was really boss.

AUTHOR
Talk about the death of the ego! That reminds me of what happened while I was writing *Tarot Revelations* with Joe. Originally it was to be a thin little book in which we both presented, in one chapter each, our two different ways of arranging the twenty-two cards of the Major Arcana. But when I saw the origin of certain of the cards in the early alchemical texts which Jung wrote about, then my part of the collaboration took a new and deeper direction, because I realized that Tarot contained the descent and ascent of Hermes/Mercurius/Thoth.

PHIL
Wouldn't that be part of what Campbell calls the monomyth, the One's descent to the material plane and his subsequent ascent?

AUTHOR
By whatever name the Avatar is known, He embodies the spiritual One. Then I discovered that the mythical stairway of planets, whereby the One and the individual soul descend and ascend, was also in the Tarot, and that led me into Gnosticism and an astrological correspondence to the Tarot.

But the death of the ego came when Joe sat down with me on one of his visits and reviewed what I had written in the interim. Page after page he drew a gigantic blue "X" across. I was crushed! And then he said, "Dick, what does this have to do with Tarot?" "Nothing," was my lame reply. "Then put it in another book."

You see I thought he was crossing out what I was saying on the basis of bad scholarship or bad writing, but all that material went into *From Eden to Eros*, for which he wrote a very nice endorsement.

ANDREW
It seems that he gave you quite a spiritual legacy, first by the collaboration on *Tarot Revelations*, and then overseeing the "rejected" material, which went into *From Eden to Eros*.

AUTHOR
But his greatest spiritual legacy was born to me *after* his death, the birth of what John Bradshaw calls the Wonder Child. Remember the writing of *The Wind and the Wizard* was a marriage of conscious and unconscious minds— hence, the sacred marriage. The divine child is the offspring of the sacred marriage. I think I have an awareness now that creativity is the most spiritual endeavor that man can pursue. Not prayers, or belief, or denial of the body, but creative play, because it is a participation *mystique* in which we in our own small way partake of the greater process whereby the Divine constantly renews and recreates the universe.

ANDREW
Have you experienced a sense of play while swimming with the dolphins?

AUTHOR
Oh, absolutely. This may be the spiritual message that they are trying to convey to us. You know in your paintings you place them around sunken pyramids and temples, in other words the religious sites of man, but it may turn out that *they* are the spiritual message-bearers for man, and that *we* have a lesson to learn from them.

ANDREW
Yes, I think so.

ARDATH
Don't forget, Richard, in "Aqueous Atlantis" the light

is coming out of the pyramid's grand passageway where the four dolphins are.

AUTHOR

Are you sure Rod and Marina didn't give you some hints about my experience with that painting.

ARDATH

No, they didn't. And when are we going to hear that story?

AUTHOR

Pretty soon I guess. I just wanted to say one more thing about Joseph Campbell, and not just what he meant to me, but what he meant to so many other people. I had the artist Jo Gill put my impression of him on the cover of *Tarot Revelations*. He is the Magus holding the lightning bolt of revelation and awakening, a Life-Changer, a Transformer. Like the Avatars, he points the way to the spiritual life, not the way of dogma and churches, but the way of the heart.

PHIL

The American Indians have always been my main interest. How did Joseph Campbell become interested in them? I mean he did grow up in New York City, did he not?

AUTHOR

New Rochelle— a suburb. Well, like my mother and father, Joe's father would take him to the American Museum of Natural History on Saturdays. They had these life-like recreations of Indian scenes. In 1910 Joe— age six— saw Buffalo Bill's Wild West Show at Madison Square Garden. When he was nine or ten, they started building a library near his house, and he used to help the men by carrying bricks to build it. Then the next year, when the library was completed, he was given a permit to roam freely in the stacks. And, he told me, "I read everything on the American Indian."

PHIL

Why do you suppose that the mythology of the Indian appealed to him over other cultures?

AUTHOR

Hmm? I never asked him that, but it's a good question. I think I know. First of all, the Indians were living their mythology, whereas the rest of Western culture had not a living mythology, but what he called a Waste Land of "collective faiths." And then secondly, the Indian mythology itself had an appreciation— more than that— a zest for life, the natural beauty of it in the sense of the Gnostic Gospel of Thomas that "the Kingdom of the Father is spread upon the earth and men do not see."

ARDATH

"I am everywhere. The earth, the sky, the water is my body."

ANDREW

The words of the Navaho Monster-Slayer.

AUTHOR

Yes, and he also acutely recognized that the American Indian had been given a raw deal by the government. In taking their land the government also psychically castrated the Indian. He wanted to champion their cause through his books, and I think he did. *The Way of the Animal Powers* has come full circle from the boy in the stacks wanting to champion the Indian cause. His mother told him about the time she took him to the movies, and in the film all these people were chasing— as he put it— "one poor little Indian, and all the audience was cheering." Joe stood up and shouted at the audience, "You've got it all wrong, you just don't understand!" He said, "My mother told me I did that, but I don't remember it." I wish he could have lived to see "Dances with Wolves." Outside of the protagonist, the only good white men in that film are dead ones.

PHIL
We'd better see what they're up to in the next room.

Phil, the Author, and Andrew and Ardath leave the library and enter the dining room. At first they are not observed by Louise, Marina, and Rod, who when he sees them abruptly stops talking.

ROD
...but we hope she's pregnant.

PHIL
Hope who's pregnant? Not my wife I hope.

Rod and Marina eye one another nervously.

LOUISE
Why don't you tell them? It's nothing to be ashamed of.

MARINA
(looking at Rod)
All right.

ROD
We hope Marina is pregnant. The medical problem is with me, not with Marina, and we asked Ratava to be a donor for artificial insemination.

AUTHOR
Why Ratava?

MARINA
Well, we did want to know who the father would be, and Ratava has qualities which if they could be passed on to a son would make an exceptional child.

ARDATH
How do you mean? As a psychic or a telepath?

MARINA
No, just as a normal person. Even when he's not speaking, he draws you into his silence, and you feel

93

elevated.

ROD
You'll see when you meet him.

LOUISE
They've also been investigating underwater birthing.

ROD
Yes, it's done in a pool with dolphins.

MARINA
They evidently send telepathic signals to the foetus of well-being, which reduce the usual anxieties experienced when leaving the safe oceanic realm of the womb.

ROD
And I think the dolphins telepathically calm the mother as well, which in turn calms the foetus, since it is an extension of the mother's body.

LOUISE
Phil went on a trip to the Soviet Union to meet Dr. Charkovsky, who is the pioneer in this field.

PHIL
He's actually not a medical doctor, but he holds an honorary doctorate in research.

ROD
Isn't he the one who has the births in the Black Sea with the dolphins in attendance?

PHIL
Some of the births did take place there, but now most of the deliveries are made in tanks in hospitals—without dolphins of course. A curious thing happened while I was visiting a museum in Leningrad called the Hermitage. I was standing in front of a tapestry that showed creatures that appeared to be a combination of dolphin and human. I didn't hear him

walk up to me, but suddenly at my side was a priest of the Russian Orthodox faith. He didn't speak very good English, and how he knew that I spoke English I'll never know, but he said, "That is fabled Atlantis, where mutations of humans to dolphins was already taking place." "To what purpose?" I asked. "To what purpose?!" he repeated, as if an answer was unnecessary. "Why, to enable those who wished to do so to survive the inevitable cataclysm." "Why inevitable?" I asked, dumbfounded at his revelation. As if he were dealing with a stupid child, he shook his head and started to walk away, then paused and said, "Inevitable because the ego places itself higher than God."

                    ARDATH
You've seen Andrew's painting, "Aqueous Atlantis."
Did the tapestry remind you of that?

                     PHIL
Not at the time, no, but now that you mention it, yes, there are similarities, except that the tapestry's dolphins are half human.

                    LOUISE
Well, if you are pregnant Marina...

SOUND OF DOORBELL

...there's the bell. Would you mind seeing who it is Phil. Marina, you must see a film on underwater birthing by Karil Daniels. She's in San Francisco, but...

A man appears with Phil in the doorway to the room. He's tall and slender, and of a dark complexion. This is the Indian Ratava. As soon as Louise, Marina, and Rod see him, their faces break into warm grins, exclaiming at once, "Ratava!"

                    RATAVA
No one at your house, and no one at the Center, so I said, "I'll bet my bottom rupee that they are with Phil and Louise." I just came down from Haleakala.

                                                    95

Small talk ensues as to when he returned, how his trip was, etc. Then he is introduced to Ardath, Andrew, and the Author. While the Author narrates, CAMERA SLOWLY CIRCLES RATAVA in conversation with the others.

                    AUTHOR
So this is Ratava. He certainly has a presence about him. I can't really put my finger on his quiet charisma, but I am certain I have a lot to learn from him in ways which are beyond the pale of intellectuality. Already questions are formulating in my mind to ask about the new relation between cetaceans and man, and what may be expected of us by them. Ratava displayed no noticeable surprise when he learned that the source of two of his telepathic receptions was not the mind of a whale but the mind of man. Phil showed him the actual Melville passage from his copy of *Moby Dick*. Quietly Marina took him aside to tell him that she would be seeing her obstetrician next week with "fingers crossed."

Next I told my story of my night in the presence of "Aqueous Atlantis." My experience was so similar to Ardath's that I was glad that she had told her story first so that mine could not be said to have been colored by her account, since I had written my experience days before hearing hers. On their way back home, Andrew and Ardath stopped at the Dolphin Center to inspect "Aqueous Atlantis." They verified that the frame had not been tampered with, and despite just hearing my story were astounded to see *Tarot Revelations* in the painting.

DISSOLVE TO EXT. OPEN OCEAN - DAY
SOUND OF WIND AND WAVES. SLOW FADE-IN to ancient ship manned by long-haired, bearded men dressed in skins.

                    AUTHOR (Narr.)
"Now when we had gone down to the ship and to the sea, first of all we drew the ship unto the fair salt water, and placed the mast and sails in the black

96

ship, and took those sheep and put them therein, and ourselves too climbed on board, sorrowing, and shedding big tears. And in the wake of our dark-prowed ship she sent a favouring wind that filled the sails, a kindly escort-even Circe of the braided tresses, a dread goddess of human speech. And we set in order all the gear throughout the ship and sat us down; and the wind and the helmsman guided our barque. And all day long her sails were stretched in her seafaring; and the sun sank and all the ways were darkened.

"She came to the limits of the world, to the deep flowing Oceanus. There is the land and the city of the Cimmerians, shrouded in mist and cloud, and never does the shining sun look down on them with his rays, neither when he climbs up the starry heavens, nor when again he turns earthward from the firmament, but deadly night is outspread over miserable mortals. Thither we came and ran the ship ashore and took out the sheep; but for our part we held on our way along the stream of Oceanus, till we came to the place which Circe had declared to us."

INT. DOLPHIN CENTER - DAY
One of the office rooms. Marina, Rod, Ratava, and the Author are gathered around a desk upon which are piles of the whale transcripts. They are talking animatedly; however we hear only SOUND OF AUTHOR'S VOICE NARRATING.

> AUTHOR (Narr.)
> In the days that followed, more and more of the transcripts yielded their sources, the most monumental of which was Homer's account of Odysseus' escape from the enchantress Circe after she had turned his men into swine and they were restored with the help of the god Hermes. They sailed to the end of the ocean where the river Styx began that went down unto hell where the ghosts of the dead walked ceaselessly. Finally I had in hand some two dozen excerpts from the finest words of man. It was time to ask some hard questions of the man who received these words, and to what purpose.

ROD
(to Ratava)
Why? What does it all mean?

MARINA
They should be out there telling one another who they
are by their songs, where the next meal is likely to be,
and who is ready for mating. Instead we get Whitman,
Milton, and now Homer.

RATAVA
Oh, there is plenty of practical talk, but it does not
take up all their time.

AUTHOR
Their time is spent in singing our songs? Why?

RATAVA
To preserve them. I am sure somewhere— perhaps
not even in the same ocean— there is another whale
singing of what happened next when Odysseus
reached the place at the end of the ocean which Circe
had declared to him. I am sure that most of the parts
of *The Odyssey* are there, and of *The Iliad* too.

ROD
If that is the case, why do you say "most of the parts
of *The Odyssey?*" Why would they leave out parts?

RATAVA
The missing parts would be missing whales.

AUTHOR
Missing whales?

RATAVA
Yes. Poisoned by pollution, or harpooned and stripped
of their flesh.

MARINA
Stripped of their flesh.

                    AUTHOR
Then, when we kill a whale, we kill a Homer, a
Melville, or....

                    MARINA
Ourselves.

                    RATAVA
Yes.

SLOW FADE OUT

EXT. DOLPHIN CENTER - DAY
Darby and Joan, the two dolphins, are frantically racing up and
down the pool, as the Author watches.

                    AUTHOR (Narr.)
In the next few weeks, some very strange things began
to happen.

Marina and Rod come to the Author's side.

                    MARINA
We just got a call from another whale-tracking station.

                    AUTHOR
Is it still happening?

                    ROD
They're all coming this way. This morning Marineland
in Honolulu released their dolphins because they
were butting their heads against the side of the pool
trying to get out.

                    MARINA
They tagged them electronically before releasing them.
Where do you suppose they headed, Richard?

                    AUTHOR
Uh, from Honolulu they would have gone south.

ROD

Right. Nineteen degrees north latitude, and one hundred fifty-eight degrees west longitude.

MARINA

They all seem to be rendezvousing about a hundred miles west of the Big Island.

AUTHOR

And last week the Panama Canal was practically clogged with whales.

ROD

I think that means that all the whales in the Atlantic Ocean have migrated to the Pacific Ocean.

MARINA

Well, there are no more Atlantic sightings of whales or dolphins, so unless they have gone to a cetacean happy-hunting ground they must be out there off Hawaii.

While they have been talking, Ratava has come out of the door from the lobby and walks up.

RATAVA

I just talked to Phil. He says that with full tanks we can easily make it to the rendezvous point and back again. Have they been tagged?

MARINA

Yes, but I hate to let them go.

Darby and Joan stop swimming at poolside next to where Marina is standing. They begin chirping to her.

MARINA

What are they thinking, Ratava?

RATAVA

(pausing)

"We go away now, but like leaving our babies behind. Heart breaking."

Marina starts crying, then Rod, and the Author.

MARINA
My heart is breaking. You are my babies too.

RATAVA
(continuing to receive the
dolphin's thoughts)
"For us name your baby Joby."

MARINA
I will! I will!

Weeping piteously she leaps into the pool, throwing her arms about the dolphins. Ratava seems strangely unmoved. Rod kneels at poolside, petting the dolphins, trying to comfort Marina.

RATAVA
(handing the Author two
packages from his pocket)
I know it is three days after Christmas, Richard, but here as a belated gift are two batteries.

AUTHOR
(puzzled)
For what?

RATAVA
You are going to take your camcorder, are you not?

AUTHOR
I guess that would be a good idea. Thank you.

RATAVA
And your batteries always go dead after five minutes, do they not?

AUTHOR
How did you *know* that?

> RATAVA
> (to Rod)
> We should have the boat gassed up in fifteen minutes.
> Then you can open the sea barrier.

Rod nods. Marina continues to hold the dolphins.

INT. AND EXT. BOAT - DAY
This is a twin-screw power launch, capable of sleeping four. It contains extensive very sophisticated electronic gear. Many of the whale song transcripts were made from this boat using hydrophones dangling in the water. SOUND OF ENGINES IDLING.

> RATAVA
> (calling to Rod and Marina)
> We'll be back before sunset! Okay, let the dolphins go.

Rod and Marina open the sea barrier and Darby and Joan streak out, pausing around the boat, chirping excitedly.

> RATAVA
> (interpreting)
> "Aren't you coming, aren't you coming?!"
> (to the Author)
> Cast off, Richard!

The boat heads out to sea.

FULL SHOT. Marina and Rod standing motionless, each with one hand raised in farewell. They gradually diminish in size as the boat pulls further away from shore.

MED SHOT
Interior boat.

> RATAVA
> Well, Richard, we have three more hours together.
> You must have many questions.

> AUTHOR
> I thought you said it is three hours out to the rendezvous point. That would make six hours.

                    RATAVA
    Yes.

                    AUTHOR
    Are we going to a mating rendezvous or what?

                    RATAVA
    A dance.

                    AUTHOR
    A what?

                    RATAVA
    We are going to a dance.

MED SHOT
Darby on the boat's portside, and Joan to starboard, are staying just
ahead of the boat.

                    RATAVA
    Do you want to take the wheel for a while. I am going
    to turn off the sonar tracking. Every once and a while
    it hits them, and it has an unpleasant effect, like
    getting zapped with electricity.

                    AUTHOR (Narr.)
    I took the wheel. It was simple to steer. If I got too close
    to Darby on the port, I corrected to the right, and vice
    versa. Watching the ocean for a time frees one of
    ordinary petty concerns, and turns the mind towards
    the depths. It is no wonder that two of our most
    profound writers were seamen, Melville and Conrad.
    One had his white whale to quest, the other his heart
    of darkness. Now, as we headed our small craft
    towards ever greater depths, I knew how Melville and
    Conrad felt watching waves roll over a watery abyss
    that opened onto seas psychic and unfathomable.

CLOSE UP
The foaming sea.

                         RATAVA
              I'll take her now, Richard.

CLOSE SHOT
The Author jumps slightly, startled.

                         AUTHOR
              My mind was somewhere else.

                         RATAVA
        It is true what you were thinking. But unfortunately
        some of the best books written by seamen never made
        it to shore, nor did their authors. Their seeing went
        too deep, and the depths they had courted wooed
        them below.

                         AUTHOR
        Yes, I had a friend like that. I guess that explains too
        why so many seamen drink. Or did drink. There
        aren't many left now. A handful can crew an entire
        ship nowadays. I guess if you can read whales' minds,
        you can read humans'.

                         RATAVA
        Yes, but it is not nearly as rewarding.

                         AUTHOR
        Do cetaceans have a mythology like man?

                         RATAVA
        Yes, there are similarities, but man fails to make the
        final connection. You know that the mythology of a
        planet is largely based upon natural phenomena.

                         AUTHOR
              What do you mean?

                         RATAVA
        In primitive Man's early mythology, there was a need
        to *understand* nature, and how Man's life fitted into
        the natural scheme.

AUTHOR

Yes, but what mythology came out of that?

RATAVA

All your mythologies, all your religions. Put yourself back in time, Richard, and you will see what I mean. You live in a cave. What is the most remarkable phenomenon every day? The sun comes up; it moves across the sky; it goes down. Will it do the same thing the next day? You don't know, do you? You hope so because all your *good* associations are with day, and all your *bad* with night. That is the basis of all your mythologies and all your religions.

AUTHOR

Night and day?

RATAVA

No, evil and good, and all of your other pairs of opposites. By day you are warm. At night you are cold. By day you are safe. At night you cannot see, but the animals can, and you may be killed. When a body is dead, it is very cold, so day and night also mean opposites of life and death, hot and cold, and bright and black; hence death and blackness are also associated with evil. Now, you also have two different kinds of people. Men and women. Man kills, woman brings forth life from her body just like the earth, so where do you put these two opposites?

AUTHOR

Woman is good, and man is evil.

RATAVA

Yes. And you make images of a woman, the goddess whom you worship in hopes of receiving good from the natural world in return for your offerings and devotion. And the goddess and her relation to you and your earth, and all that comes out of its body and lives upon it, is the spiritual impetus of life on earth until 1200 B.C. as you point out in your book *From Eden to Eros*. By the way, Richard, Marina loaned this book

105

to me and I think you understand, with Joseph Campbell's great help....

AUTHOR

Indeed.

RATAVA

...why the new religion failed in no longer honoring the earth and all its creatures. You were now in a covenant with an angry male god, who gave you dominion over the earth, to kill and rape. And you yourself rightly saw this as an outgrowth of new patriarchal, warrior societies utilizing weapons of iron; hence the name Iron Age. Societal and ecological war became the order of the day. Fire had been tamed, and now was used also as a weapon— like iron— to overcome others. Now here is an important distinction between man's present patriarchal religions— Christianity, Judaism, and Islam— and the earlier goddess religions which you did *not* make in your book. And you should have.

AUTHOR

I'm all ears.

RATAVA

Like the body of the earth that gave birth to all things, the peoples born of the goddess' womb— everywoman's— were sacred. No distinction was made between *your* people and other people, whereas *now* to be a Jew you have to be born of a Jewish mother. If you are not, you cannot be a Jew, and you are "the other." Not of us. Not we the chosen people. Therefore you can be killed. Our covenant with our god says so. He even encourages us to war in his name— Islam. So do you wonder that your planet is in such a mess with such a mythology, Richard?

AUTHOR

No, we have created what we deserve.

106

RATAVA

You see in the goddess religion, not to see the sacred origins of another person— no matter what tribe— is to profane your own existence and that of your whole tribe. So you have cooperation among peoples, and what is the corollary in relation to the earth?

AUTHOR

Nurturing.

RATAVA

Exactly. Now all that remained for the new religion was to "put down"— as you said— the old religion, which involved denigrating woman and the serpent. On that day that I met you at Phil's house, I had been at the astronomical observatory on Hawaii. I was looking at the serpent through the telescope, and at the star Eltanin which you said represented the goddess— our Eve— to the people of her religion. Then I meditated, and I was able to get into the frame of mind of those times. I can tell you the difference is like that between night and day.
(laughter)

AUTHOR
(laughter)
If only man had blamed things on the night instead of women and nature....

RATAVA

Planets that do not have such natural phenomena as yours might not have such a mythology, don't you think?

AUTHOR

Yes, it would be nice to visit a planet without a myth of good or evil.

RATAVA

There are such places.

Did none of the religions try to dissolve the pairs of opposites or see through them?

RATAVA

Well, yes. As primitive man observed nature he saw that the animals were driven by the same overwhelming sex drive that he himself experienced. The association of sex and birth was very long in coming, because the offspring of the act was very long in coming.

The ways of the West are to bang heads, lock horns, confront something head on, which is exemplified in the put down of the earlier goddess religions by patriarchy, which you wrote about. The ways of the East are more subtle, as in the martial arts, where the energy of the attacker is utilized by the defender to work against the aggressor. In this same way, the discipline of Tantra rode the so-called— in the West— base animal desire to the heights of spiritual ecstasy. A union or yoga with the divine was attained. Such a concept is heretical not only in deed but also in thought in the West. During the time in the West of severe religious persecutions, Tantra found its way into your culture in a somewhat— shall we say— disguised form. Alchemy. The question you asked me was "Did none of the religions try to *dissolve* the pairs of opposites?" "*Solve et coagula.*" You remember that Latin term from your collaboration with Joseph Campbell? The goal of alchemy was the resolution of all pairs of opposites. It was in truth a religion— in answer to your question— and hence its spiritual truth was grasped intuitively by a man of such great spiritual stature as Jung, who also saw in it a depth psychology incorporating the divine. Tantra and alchemy refined the base metal of patriarchal pairs of opposites by incorporating the divine through a fifth element which resolved not only two pairs of opposites but also two more, which came from the recognition that the earth plane had four quarters or directions, and, therefore, a *season* for each quarter where the life principle, the sun, resided. At the same time, four elements were recognized, earth, air, fire, and water, in the natural world. The fifth element, which may be thought of as a circle at the center of a square, involves the devotee to the extent that he or she is now at the center of the cosmos, and there, of course, is the divine also. The separation of the divine and his creation, man, is the most foolish of all the features of your mythologies.

Which brings me to the answer to your question, "Do cetaceans have a mythology like man?" I replied that there were similarities, "but man fails to make the final connection." It is very difficult for you to do, because man sees himself not only as separate from his creator, but also fallen, base, worthless, sinful, guilty. If God is day and the light, you are evil darkness and the night.

But let us say that a dietary indiscretion did not result in the Fall of Man. Eve did *not* eat the apple, and Man remained in the Garden with some of the goodness of the Creator in him despite having been made of base clay. Where then does your mythology go from there?

AUTHOR
Nowhere.

RATAVA
Exactly.

AUTHOR
Because there can be no drama, no progression, only stasis.

RATAVA
Quite right. Now here is where Man fails to make the final connection. The Divine is immanent in its creation. This simple idea is known on practically every planet throughout the cosmos. How could it be otherwise? However, Man who sees himself as the center of the cosmos, through his religions, a cosmos

void of other intelligent beings, whereby he is the intellectual giant at its center judging all the far-flung galaxies. What a vainglorious and sorry spectacle!

Now I know you do not think that way yourself, Richard, and if you did think that way Joseph Campbell would have kicked you out upon the occasion of your first meeting. Instead, you were friends from then until his death. And, as far as I am concerned, if you thought that way, I would not have invited you to the dance.

AUTHOR
What dance? You said that before.

RATAVA
You shall see soon enough. But you would have missed it right enough if I had not given you the new batteries for your camera. You are very good with the intuition but not so good with the sensation.

AUTHOR
Resolution of the pairs of opposites is what it is all about.

RATAVA
And study won't help you with sensation. You have to keep stubbing your toe on dead batteries. But back to the "final connection," Richard. If the divine is imma-nent in its creation, then in the *act* of creation the divine participates. For Me, for you. Time is the act of divine creation, not the stasis of the Eden Garden. As time expands, so does the creations that flow out of it. What is another word for "acting," Richard?

AUTHOR
(reflecting)
To play a part?

RATAVA
"Play" will suffice. To act is to play at a role or a part, because we say it is pretend, not reality— the real man

being behind the mask of the actor. Richard, listen to me! If you accept that the divine participates when you create, then *play* is the highest spiritual act that man can attain. But when you grow up, you also murder how to play. Think about it. What man today calls play is not play at all, but a fierce competition that is but a mirror of the activities which consume him in getting to work, the work place, and in his personal relations. Getting there, making it is the collective goal of man. Take sports as an example. Again only fierce competition. True play has no goal, no structure, and like creation, is an on-going process of self-discovery.

Even now, the One is playing at being you and Me. In all the *material* universes, there is *one* myth of the descent of spirit to matter and the subsequent ascent. The One coming down the Tree or Pole at the center of the four quarters of the earth. And up again along that fifth element that incorporates the human, and by so doing, *unites* Above and Below, God and man, wave and particle. Even in terms of your primitive physics, there is a simultaneity between wave and particle, unmanifest and manifest, in a "Now you see it, now you don't" divine dance.

AUTHOR
Are you talking about the electron that appears to jump instantaneously from one ring of an atom to another? When we don't see the electron, we assume it is in its wave form.

RATAVA
Yes...and no. You see, like the Divine it is always a wave, always spirit. But it can choose to clothe itself in matter and become a particle as part of its divine play. The message which the cetaceans bring to Man is "play creatively," or, "create playfully." Why, Richard? Because you, and the planet, and the Divine are in a mutual dance of creation. That is the final connection that the cetaceans make, and Man does not.

111

AUTHOR

I've had a feeling that you know the sources of the other whale songs that I failed to identify. Do the whales have other songs about their own myths?

RATAVA

They have myths of the four elements, as you do here on earth. That is, fire, air, earth, and water.

AUTHOR

Tell me about these myths, please.

RATAVA

The Fire Time is their oldest myth, about a time when they lived on a very distant planet.

AUTHOR

What?!

RATAVA

Yes, at this time their planet was undergoing volcanism. Eruptions of fiery lava necessitated their leaving the planet. They were then mammals with bodies not unlike modern man, except for the huge bulging heads to contain their massive brains. In technology and the extent of their civilization they were far beyond earth's present development.

AUTHOR

How did they leave their planet?

RATAVA

In circular-shaped crafts propelled by electro-magnetic forces.

AUTHOR

Flying saucers!

RATAVA

When the craft entered the vicinity of a planet's field, scanners on the craft determined whether or not the atmosphere was suitable for air-breathing mammalian life. If not the long journey continued with everyone aboard in a state of suspended animation.

AUTHOR

Frozen?

RATAVA

Yes, but capable of being revived once a planet with the proper atmosphere was reached.

AUTHOR

And that planet was earth?

RATAVA

Yes, that was many millions of years ago. The long journey through space is referred to as the Air Time. They were not vegetables, as you would say today, during their long period of unconsciousness. Pre-programmed stimulation of the neo-cortex took place, and, therefore, their brains continued to grow. The Air Time is also known by another name, the same which the aborigines use, The Dream Time.

AUTHOR

From what constellation did they come?

RATAVA

By what you, Richard, would call a synchronicity, they came from Cetus, the Whale. Am I correct in saying that Jung attributed no cause to the phenomenon of synchronicity?

AUTHOR

Yes, at least he said "acausal."

RATAVA

But you yourself attribute a cause to synchronicity?

AUTHOR

Well, I don't believe that Jung amplified on it further for fear of being labelled even more of a mystic than he already was regarded. Certainly he meant that there was no causal relation in the material sequence of events proceeding the synchronicity.

RATAVA

Yes, and what do *you* think, Richard?

AUTHOR

Well, I think that the *mind* influences events, thereby *psychically* causing synchronicities. Joseph Campbell and I attended a conference at the Menninger Institute in Council Groves, Kansas, where I gave a lecture on "Psychic Cause and Effect."

RATAVA

Well, you're right. Mostly however human beings affect their lives in a negative way to bring out unhappy situations. Why is that more prevalent than bringing about good times? Because the power of hate and anger is now much greater in the human.

AUTHOR

What was life like here on the planet when they landed?

RATAVA

Problems were considerable because of the extreme size and aggression of the ruling species, the dinosaur, which possessed the same reptilian brain as in the ancestry of the human, which perhaps answers yet again why hate and anger are more compelling emotions in your species. But to return to the early problems, conscious life amounted to only about an hour a day during the first few months here, making some easy prey while immobile and still "dreaming," as you would call it. In a certain sense, the dreaming kept them in contact with their spiritual source, out of which all matter evolves.

AUTHOR

How could they land if they were still in suspended animation?

RATAVA

When the craft's scanners indicated a favorable plan-
etary atmosphere, then computerized control of the
craft went into the landing phase.

AUTHOR

But what must it have been like living on this planet
with all their intelligence, yet facing the prospect of
being eaten by a dinosaur at any moment!

RATAVA

Quiet horrific. This was the beginning of the Earth
Time. The One Myth told of the Spirit, the All-Creating
Divine Principle present in every materialization of
matter; hence, they could not kill the dinosaurs,
since they themselves were after all manifestations—
however unevolved— of the One. Incidentally, your
biblical Hell has its origins in the myth of The Fire
Time.

AUTHOR

You mean that *our* religions are influenced by these
myths?

RATAVA

Of course. Remember again, Richard, there is basically only One Myth no matter what name is given
to it. The One descends to matter.

AUTHOR

What about Hinduism?

RATAVA

The All-Devouring Kali who laps up blood with her
long tongue reminds you of a carnivorous dinosaur,
does she not? But the horrific aspects of early life
during the Earth Time came to be all but forgotten
during the last elemental period, the Water Time,
when the extra-terrestrial ancestors of the Cetaceans
consciously decided to leave the land for life in the
sea. There was a long, very peaceful and benign time
until Kali and the horrific aspect of life on earth once

more reared its head in the form of whalers who harpooned the hapless whales and then stripped the flesh from the bone with long flensing knives.

AUTHOR
My god, that really makes us appear to be bloody savages.

RATAVA
And so you are. But in the myths of the One, ultimate salvation is possible, and Whale Song myth is no different in that respect from human myth of the return of the Avatar or Savior. Cetaceans sing of the Second Coming of the Pod, the craft which carried them here during the Air Time, but also the name of a cetacean family.

AUTHOR
The Second Coming of a Savior in human mythology is to resurrect the dead, or to save the faithful in peril.

RATAVA
Precisely. When the cetaceans are in peril of being a species no more, or when their environment undergoes transformations endangering their survival, their myth which they sing in their Whale Song says that the Cosmic Pod will return for them, its portals will open once again and flood with water, purified instantaneously of man's pollutants, and they shall swim in. Then the portals will close, the Pod ascend, and a new cycle of Dream Time will begin, with a new home to be found.

AUTHOR
Where will they go?

RATAVA
Only the One knows.

The Author is silent now, musing on the ramifications of Ratava's words.

116

AUTHOR

Will there be no cetaceans on earth?

RATAVA

None.

AUTHOR

Are they leaving now?

RATAVA

Yes.

AUTHOR

Why?

RATAVA

Earth is a dying planet.

AUTHOR

Why?

RATAVA

Polluted. Every moment toxic wastes dumped into the ocean are breaking free— like the genie in the bottle. And you cannot put this genie back into the bottle because you cannot retrieve the containers of waste from the bottom of the ocean. You humans have wasted your planet. When you first began to think that you were no longer caretakers of the Garden, but could own it, you began to destroy it.

AUTHOR

What garden?

RATAVA

The Garden of Eden— Earth. The Serpent in the Garden was not evil, but the essence of the Great Spirit, The One.

AUTHOR

I know.

RATAVA

But your friend Campbell said it most succinctly.
"Wherever nature is revered as self-moving, and so
inherently divine, the serpent is revered as symbolic
of its divine life. And accordingly, in the Book of
Genesis, where the serpent is cursed, all nature is
devaluated, and its power of life regarded as nothing
in itself." And so you see, Richard, humanity set up
instead a god of your own creation, and of the creation
of the authors of the bible.

AUTHOR

I know. I said in my book *From Eden to Eros* the
"victory of Yahweh will have repercussions down to
our present day in areas as seemingly unrelated to
the Garden of Eden as ecology."

RATAVA

You see now— I hope— that the Earth is the Garden of
Eden. That bible gave man what was called dominion
over nature, but it really was a mandate for rape.

FULL SHOT
A mile ahead of the boat, the tall dorsal fins of Orcas can be seen
dipping in and out of the water.

RATAVA

I see the dance is already beginning.

AUTHOR

What dance?! What are you talking about?

The author looks in the direction of Ratava's gaze. Plumes of spray
from whales intermingle with the Orcas.

RATAVA

Phil told you a little about Wovoka and the Ghost
Dance.

AUTHOR

Yes.

118

RATAVA

He did not tell you the climax of the dance.

AUTHOR

No.

RATAVA

In 1889, many Indians came to hear Wovoka speak of the Coming of the Messiah. They brought back to their own tribes his words and the instructions for Ghost Dancing. They were to join hands in a circle and dance all night— sometimes six straight nights— in a west to east direction to bring about the resurrection of their people, and the disappearance of the White Man in a natural catastrophe. But there would have been no tragedy as a result of the Ghost Dance had not there been repeated broken promises by the government to the Sioux nation, which numbered 25,000 people in 1890. And hunger, hunger, hunger. At this time an Indian who did not stay on his assigned reservation was regarded as hostile and could be killed on sight. Indeed, those who would not go to the reservations were branded hostiles and hunted down by cavalry. Without the buffalo to hunt, the Indians depended upon the promises of the government for food. By 1889, the beef ration had been reduced by more than one-half in three years. In 1890, the government agent at the Pine Ridge Sioux reservation complained to Washington that the treaty called for 470,400 pounds of beef as the April ration, and only 205,000 pounds had been given. He was told that it was better to issue half rations all the time, than full rations at the beginning and none for the rest of the year. In October Sitting Bull broke the peace pipe he had smoked with the White Man.

The boat has now reached the outer perimeter of the whales and orcas, which seem to be swimming in vast circles. Ratava cuts the engine to idle. Darby and Joan seem torn between joining the other dolphins, cavorting among the orcas and whales, and staying with the boat. Despite the normally friendly nature of cetaceans, it is as if the tensions contained in Ratava's account of Pine Ridge have become conveyed to the whales and orcas, some of which pass dangerously close to the boat, often rolling partially out of the water as they pass to cast a baleful eye upon the boat's occupants. Ratava does not seem to notice the potential menace from the cetaceans. MONTAGE OF CETACEANS PASSING BOAT while he continues his narrative.

RATAVA

In December, 1890, upon learning that he was to be arrested, Sitting Bull decided to flee the reservation with his family. In the ensuing fight, Sitting Bull and his son Crow Foot, 17, were killed. Thus died one of the greatest medicine men of the Teton Sioux. He was not a chief but a shaman, who became a warrior out of necessity, participating in the battle of Little Big Horn whereby Custer's command was wiped out of existence.

The frenzied swimming of the cetaceans around the boat increases.

RATAVA

For seven years he opposed the treaty by which the great Sioux reservation was at last broken up in 1890. When asked by a White Man what the Indians thought of it, he said, "Indians! There are no Indians left now but me!" After the death of Sitting Bull, the only leader outside of the Bad Lands, where the hostiles lived, regarded as dangerous was Big Foot. Four hundred and seventy troops, armed with light artillery, were sent to Big Foot's camp at Wounded Knee creek on December 29, 1890. The Indians wore sacred red paint and "ghost shirts" under their clothing which Short Bull and other medicine men who had visited Wovoka had told them would render harmless the bullets of the White Men. They had been Ghost Dancing to no avail for nearly a year now to bring back the dead buffalo and to resurrect all the tribes of dead Indians.

Now there is an occasional thump as a whale or orca bumps the side of the boat. The Author is becoming increasingly alarmed, but Ratava quietly continues his narrative.

120

RATAVA
The first volley of artillery trained on the camp at
Wounded Knee sent a storm of shells among the
women and children gathered in front of the tipis to
watch the grand spectacle of military display. Some
dead were pursued as far as two miles away. All told
about 300 men, women, and children died, and that
was the end of the Ghost Dancing. Now 100 years and
a day have passed since then. The Ghost Dance is
about to begin again. You had better say goodbye now
to Darby and Joan, Richard. They are waiting to join
the other cetaceans in the dance. And when you have
finished saying goodbye, get your camera for this will
be like nothing else the world has seen.

The Author moves to the rail of the boat, where Darby and Joan have
been standing on their tails looking in. He strokes their beaks, lowers
his head so that they can nuzzle him, and then after chirping some
words he cannot understand, they swim off. An inner circle of
dolphins parts to admit Darby and Joan. This circle is swimming
slowly from right to left. Just outside of the circle of dolphins, orcas
swim in another circle. At the periphery of circles are the whales, all
sizes and species. The Author has trained his camcorder upon the
cetaceans.

RATAVA
When Wovoka went up to heaven to God, he was also
given incantations to chant during the Ghost Dance.
He remembered the Dance, but not the chants. That
is why the Ghost Dance did not succeed then. Now it
will.

Ratava begins chanting in various Indian dialects, which are translated into English by subtitles. The first dialect in which Ratava
begins chanting is Cheyenne. The three circles of dolphins, orcas and
whales continue to swim in a sunwise direction.

RATAVA
I bring you a holy arrow,
Says the Father,
Says the Father.
From the Spirit of the Air,

Says the Father,
Says the Father,
From the Eagle in the North
Says the Father,
Says the Father,
To the Cheyenne below
Says the Father
Says the Father.

Now Ratava speaks in English to the cetaceans.

Sing my children!

At his words the three circles of cetaceans have begun to slow their swimming. First the dolphins "stand" in the water, their fins touching, and begin to repeat verbatim the Cheyenne words for "Says the Father" which Ratava has chanted. Soon the orcas are also standing in the water and chanting in their deeper bass. The whale song also commences with the "Says the Father" chorus of the chant, by the end of which all the cetaceans are chanting in unison. The Author is filming with his camcorder.

RATAVA
I am certainly glad, Richard, that I brought those extra batteries for you.

AUTHOR
(without looking up)
I am too, but the microphone doesn't translate. Would you translate for me?

RATAVA
The People are being called. All of the Indians from the last four elemental Ages on earth. The caretakers of the Garden are called to resurrection at the end of each elemental age of Water on earth. Water signifies baptism in the Great Spirit. The last time the caretaking people were called on earth was some eight thousand years ago at the end of the Cancerian era.

Now the cetaceans begin singing a new song which is translated in sub-titles as follows:

CETACEANS
The Father comes from above,
The Father comes from above,
From the home of the Spirit-host above,
From the home of the Spirit-host above.
See! The Eagle comes,
Says the Father.
Now at last we see him,
Says the Father.
Look! Look! The Eagle comes,
Says the Father.
Now we see him with the People,
Says the Father.

Far above, the morning star, Mercury, seems to shine brighter. All the cetaceans have their heads turned to look above, but the Author does not see this.

AUTHOR
They're not singing now what you chanted.

RATAVA
No, my chant was the first element— Air— of the four elemental incantations brought back from heaven by Wovoka for the Ghost Dance. Air, or Gemini, was the first of the last four elemental ages, from six to four thousand B.C. During that time the Indian People were descending from the north, from Canada and Alaska, from the direction of the land bridge from Asia over which they had crossed. The Cheyenne are the tribe of the north, and the talisman for their resurrection is the sacred medicine arrow, adorned with feathers from the sacred bird of the element Air, the eagle.

AUTHOR
How do the cetaceans know the words?

RATAVA
Really, Richard, the ego of the white man knows no bounds. Do you think only your songs are worthy of being remembered and sung by cetaceans? These are

the songs of the Indian people, sung by cetaceans since their creation.

> CETACEANS
> Father, the Morning Star!
> Father, the Morning Star!
> Look on us, we have danced until daylight,
> Look on us, we have danced until daylight,
> Take pity on us— Hi'i'i'!
> Take pity on us— Hi'i'i'!
>
> It is your father coming,
> It is your father coming,
> A spotted eagle is coming for you,
> A spotted eagle is coming for you.

Now the brightness of the descending "morning star" has increased.

> AUTHOR
> What are they singing now?

> RATAVA
> (looking above)
> They address the Great Spirit in the morning star. You know it as the planet Mercury, ruler of the Air sign Gemini. They are saying that they have been ghost dancing all night to bring about their salvation, and they ask their Father in the morning star to take pity upon them.

The glow on the cetaceans from the "morning star" is now so bright that even the Author can see it through the viewfinder of his camcorder. He looks above to where there is a glowing space-craft hovering about 1000 feet up. As he watches, a gigantic feathered arrow materializes in the northern quarter of the sky.

> RATAVA
> (addressing the cetaceans,
> with arms raised)
> I bring you a clay pipe,
> Says the Father,
> Says the Father,

From the Spirit of the Earth,
Says the Father,
Says the Father,
From the Serpent in the South
Says the Father,
Says the Father,
To the Crow below,
Says the Father,
Says the Father.

Sing, my children!

All the cetaceans begin chanting "Says the Father." Ratava's chant has been in the Crow dialect. When Ratava has finished chanting, he turns to the Author.

RATAVA
The second of the four elemental ages is Earth or Taurus, ruled by the evening star, Venus. Between four and two thousand B.C. the People streamed south across the Great Plains into Mexico and central America, and founded the great culture of the Mayans. The Crow are the tribe of the South and the talisman for the resurrection of the People of the South is the clay pipe, made from the element Earth, wherein lives the sacred serpent of the Garden.

CETACEANS
I bring you a pipe,
I bring you a pipe,
Says the Father,
Says the Father,
By means of it you shall live again,
By means of it you shall live again,
Says the Father,
Says the Father.

The whole world is coming,
A Nation is coming,
The Eagle has brought the message to the
People,
The Father says so.

125

Over the whole earth they are coming
The buffalo are coming,
The Crow has brought the message to the
People,
The Father says so.

The Father will descend,
The Father will descend,
The earth will tremble,
The earth will tremble,
Everyone will arise,
Everyone will arise,
Stretch out your hands,
Stretch out your hands.

At the last line, "Stretch out your hands," the dolphins and orcas make an exaggerated effort to touch flippers with one another. Overhead, in the southern quarter of the sky, a beautiful clay pipe materializes, from the bowl of which smoke rises above.

RATAVA
The Great Spirit draws the first puff of smoke.

The Author has seen the manifestation and pointed his camcorder above.

AUTHOR
Damn! I need to replace the battery.

RATAVA
Fortunately for me, it is not your damnation. There are the other batteries which I brought you.

The Author in his haste nearly slips and falls.

RATAVA
No reason for haste. It will not go away.

Now the cetaceans are silent. Presently one dolphin squeaks out a few short syllables, followed by similar but not alike sounds from other dolphins. When the dolphins have concluded, the orcas begin, followed by the whales.

126

AUTHOR
What's going on now?

RATAVA
They are singing the names of the "Little Christs."

AUTHOR
Who are the "Little Christs?"

RATAVA
The three hundred and sixty Indian men, women, and children murdered by the white soldiers at Wounded Knee. There is a name for every one of the three hundred and sixty degrees of the great circle of the sky.

AUTHOR
Why are they named now?

RATAVA
They shall be called first.

Now Ratava turns his back on the Author, and moves once more to the forward end, where he begins chanting in Sioux dialect, his arms upraised to the sky.

RATAVA
I bring you a feathered pipe,
Says the Father,
Says the Father,
From the Spirit of the Fire,
Says the Father,
Says the Father,
From the Buffalo in the West,
Says the Father,
Says the Father,
To the Sioux below,
Says the Father,
Says the Father.

Again the cetaceans chorus "Says the Father," etc. Suddenly high above in the western sky, a feathered pipe appears.

RATAVA
(to the Author)
White Buffalo Cow Woman brought the holy pipe to
the Sioux so that they could send their voices on the
smoke to Grandfather and Father "Wakan-Tanka,"
the Cosmic Buffalo who stands at the gate of the
setting sun through which all animals come forth
onto the earth, and through which they return to be
reborn after death.

Simultaneous with Ratava's explanation to the Author, the cetaceans begin singing.

CETACEANS
The spirit host is advancing,
Says the Father,
Says the Father,
They are coming with the buffalo,
Says the Father,
Says the Father,
They are coming with the new earth,
Says the Father,
Says the Father.

RATAVA
(to the Author)
White Buffalo Cow Woman gave the feathered pipe to
a Sioux chief with these words, "With this sacred pipe
you will walk upon the Earth, your Grandmother and
Mother. Every step taken upon her should be as a
prayer. The red-stone pipe bowl is the Earth. The
buffalo calf carved upon it represents the creatures
that live upon your Mother. The stem of wood signifies
the trees and all that grows upon Her. The twelve
feathers hanging from where the stem meets the bowl
shall remind you constantly of the union of heaven
and earth in the tree and its roots, for the feathers are
from the spotted eagle who lives both in heaven and
earth. When you smoke this sacred pipe, all elements
of the universe are joined with you and lift their voices
to Wakan-Tanka."

CETACEANS
(simultaneously with
Ratava's following words)
I shall cut off his feet,
I shall cut off his feet,
I shall cut off his head,
I shall cut off his head.
He gets up again.
He gets up again.

RATAVA
When Buffalo Woman left the sacred pipe, she left the earth, saying "I am leaving, but remember, in me there are four ages. I shall look back upon your people and shall return at the end.

AUTHOR
The four elemental ages of 8,000 years?

RATAVA
Yes. The third is the Fire Age of Aries, ruled by Mars, from 2,000 B.C. to the birth of Christ. From his nostrils the Cosmic Buffalo breathes smoke and fire of the Great Spirit. He is Wakan-Tanka. He incarnates in the flesh of the buffalo to feed his people. "This is My Body and My Blood." There would be no reason to resurrect the people with the Ghost Dance if the buffalo herds did not come back to life again to feed the people. He is the sacrifice of the Eucharist offered to his People.

CETACEANS
(following Ratava's words)
Now He is walking,
Now He is walking,
Grandfather Buffalo is walking,
Father Buffalo is walking,
They are opening the Gate of the Dead,
They are opening the Gate of the Dead,
Says the Father.
Says the Father.

In the southwest, a fiery red buffalo appears simultaneously with another in the northwest. They turn right and left respectively, bobbing their heads up and down as if pushing an object. No sooner have they done this than the breadth of the western horizon reddens remarkably, appearing at first to be a sunset, but then an immense herd of red buffalo are revealed stretching from north to south. They gallop up towards the "Morning Star" craft which is still hovering above, narrowing gradually to the width of a red beam which enters the craft and vanishes. Now, from amid the clouds of this lofty gate, the People begin to materialize, marching steadily towards the east. As they go, the ranks behind them are continuously filled by those pouring through the gate. They pass overhead covering the sky between the craft and the ocean. Now they stand motionless with their backs to our perspective, facing the east. Ratava begins chanting in Arapaho dialect.

RATAVA
(to the sky, arms upraised)
I bring you a blue cloud hail,
Says the Father,
Says the Father,
From the Spirit of the Water,
Says the Father,
Says the Father,
From the Whale in the East,
Says the Father,
Says the Father,
To the Arapaho below,
Says the Father,
Says the Father,
Whereby you shall all live again.

Again the cetaceans chorus "Says the Father," but adding each time, "whereby you shall all live again." Over the People standing in the East a blue cloud forms.

RATAVA
(to the Author)

The last elemental age is Water, the sign of Pisces, from the birth of Christ until now, when the four ages end and another of 8,000 years commences. The Arapaho are the People of the East, where the rising

130

sun of resurrection is born. They are called the Blue Cloud People. The Morning Star in the East is Jupiter.

CETACEANS

My children, my children,
It is I who wear the morning star on my head,
It is I who wear the morning star on my head,
I show it to my children,
I show it to my children,
Says the Father,
Says the Father.

A bright star appears in the east and descends into the blue cloud.

RATAVA
(to the author)
The Angel of the Evangelist, clothed in cloud.

A blue, very gentle hail begins falling, whereupon some of the People begin ascending, moving backwards up towards the craft at a 45 degree angle as if drawn by a ray.

AUTHOR
Are there no white men?

RATAVA
No. The White Man cannot ascend, for he was not a caretaker of the Garden. The Red Man hunted all the earth's creatures, and yet returned them to the Great Spirit, and kept the Great Spirit in his heart and blessed the earth as he walked upon it. The White Man hunted all the creatures too; yet paid no homage unto their death, and made a great fire from the atom to consume all his brethren.

The blue hail increases, and more and more of the People are drawn up to the Pod.

CETACEANS
All of our People are going up,
All of our People are going up,
Above to where the Father dwells,

131

"Luminous Ascension"
by Andrew Annenberg

Above to where the Father dwells,
Above to where our People live,
Above to where our People live.

We shall live again,
We shall live again,
Says the Father,
Says the Father.

All of the People have been taken up into the Pod. A turtle surfaces in the center of the circle of dolphins, bearing on its back mud and a small tree growing up from the center of its shell.

> RATAVA
> Now there is a center for the four quarters, and earth for the Pod to land.

The white light of Jupiter, the Morning Star, detaches itself from the Blue Cloud above and descends to hover over the boat.

> RATAVA
> One White Man is called.

Suddenly Joseph Campbell appears, seemingly standing a few feet over the water to the right of the boat. The Author sees him and exclaims:

> AUTHOR
> Joe!

> RATAVA
> He cannot hear you; he is still in Spirit.

The Blue Cloud hail begins falling about Joseph Campbell.

> RATAVA
> The People themselves have called Joseph Campbell as their champion. He has met many Indians in Spirit, and he was himself an Indian many times before his last life.

Joseph Campbell begins to slowly ascend towards the Pod.

Joe!   (to Ratava)
Can he hear me now?!

RATAVA
He can hear you, but he does not wish to speak with
a White Man's voice. At the end, White Man's words
caught in his craw. No he wishes Chief Seattle of the
Suquamish to speak for him and all the People. It is
a message for all who would become Caretakers of the
Garden again.

As Ratava speaks in Suquamish dialect, Campbell continues to
ascend as the blue hail continues falling.

RATAVA
The President in Washington sends word that he
wishes to buy our land, but how can you buy or sell
the sky and land. Every part of the earth is sacred to
our people. Every shining pine needle, every sandy
shore, every mist in the dark woods, every meadow.
We know the sap which courses through the trees as
we know the blood that courses through our veins.
The shining water that moves in the streams is not
just water, but the blood of our ancestors. If we sell
you our land, remember that it is sacred. Each
ghostly reflection in the clear water of the lakes tells
of events and memories in the life of our people. The
water's murmur is the voice of our father's father. So
if we sell you our land, you must keep it apart and
sacred, as a place where man can go to taste the wind
that is sweetened by the meadow flowers. Will you
teach your children what we have taught our children? That the earth is our mother and that what
befalls the earth, befalls all the sons of earth. This we
know: the earth does not belong to man. Man belongs
to the earth. All things are connected like the blood
which unites us all. Man did not weave the web of life,
he is merely a strand in it. Whatever he does to the
web, he does to himself. One thing we know: to harm
the earth or its creatures is to heap contempt upon its
creator. When the last Red Man has vanished with his

wilderness and his memory is only the shadow of a cloud moving across the prairie, will these forests still be here? Will there be left any of the spirit of our people. We love this earth as a newborn loves its mother's heartbeat. So if we sell you our land, love it as we have loved it. Care for it as we have cared for it. Hold in your mind the memory of the land as it is when you receive it. Preserve the land for all children and love it, as God loves us all.

Joseph Campbell, like all of the Indians before him, has been absorbed into the Pod on a ray. Now the Pod begins descending.

CETACEANS
The mountain, the mountain, It is circling around, It is circling around.

The Pod lands on the water; its portals open, and the inner circle of dolphins swim in.

AUTHOR
How can the Pod take all those dolphins?!

RATAVA
You might call it "miniaturization." We call it "micronization." One dolphin will become no bigger than a computer chip; then it will be placed in suspended animation for the long voyage.

MED SHOT
A shower of spray emits from the Pod as the salt water is blown out by air tanks. Then the portals open again and the entire circle of orcas swim in. The above procedure is repeated, and as the circle of whales begins entering the Pod, the Author says to Ratava:

AUTHOR
I wish I could go with them.

RATAVA
I can, but you must show the world what you have seen so that the old mistakes are not repeated again.

As Ratava speaks, his body begins to undergo a transformation, the shoulders bulging and moving upwards toward the head, until there is no longer a neck, and the arms shrivel, becoming flippers. The head bulges at the forehead, and the prominent beak of a dolphin extrudes from where his nose has been. As his lower body begins its transformation, he waddles uncertainly to the boat's fantail, where he pauses, then speaks in a voice half-human, half-dolphin.

RATAVA

Goodbye, Rich-ard.

Then his two legs grow together, culminating where his feet have been in a flipper. Arching his back, he flips backwards over the fantail into the water. Coming up, he blows a fountain of spray from his blow hole, then he rolls onto one side, casting a long look at the Author while waving a flipper, then he swims into the Pod. The last portal closes; the air tanks purge the sea water; and the Pod slowly ascends, where it hovers while the Author starts the boat's engines.

FULL SHOT
AS THE AUTHOR SPEAKS, CAMERA PULLS UP AND BACK TO GRADUALLY ENCOMPASS THE POD, THE BOAT, AND THE NOW EMPTY OCEAN. IN THE SKY, THE MANIFESTATIONS AT THE FOUR QUARTERS BEGIN TO FADE, WHILE THE POD GLOWS LIKE THE MORNING STAR.

AUTHOR (Narr.)

Marina's gestation period was one year. She gave birth in the pool at the Dolphin Center as Ratava had instructed her. Her offspring were not human and not dolphin, but male and female of a new species that would perhaps save the world at last.

THE POD GLOWS BRILLIANTLY, THEN ASCENDS RAPIDLY AS THE BOAT BECOMES BUT A TINY SPECK, ULTIMATELY DISAPPEAR-ING AS CAMERA ZOOMS INTO SPACE TO PRESENT FIRST A VIEW OF THE ENTIRE HAWAIIAN ISLAND CHAIN, NORTH AND SOUTH AMERICA, THEN ONE HALF OF PLANET EARTH. SOUND OF RATAVA'S VOICE:

RATAVA

"The earth, the sky, the water is my body, and the seasons too. But don't think that I am just in the east, south, west, or north, or under the earth, or up in the sky. I am everywhere."

SLOW FADE OUT

136

ANDREW ANNENBERG

Andrew Annenberg was born in Santa Monica on September 25, 1945. In his early youth the family moved to Washington, D.C., and it was there that Andrew visited the Smithsonian, which would have a major impact on his career. Awed by the vast collection of masterpieces, young Andrew made repeated visits to this renowned Institute, and began drawing at the age of seven.

In 1961, after returning to California, Andrew began oil painting, and was admitted as the youngest member to the Santa Monica Art Association. After graduating from Santa Monica High, Andrew took many city college art courses, finally progressing to a rigorous discipline of self-teaching. In 1965 Andrew won first place for California in the National Society for Arts & Letters, and went on to become a first runner-up in the Nationals. Emulating Thoreau, he then moved to an island in Washington State where he could paint directly from nature. Since 1974 he has resided on Maui in the Hawaiian Islands.

An Annenberg show entitled "Revelations" at the Aspen Art Museum inspired the reviewer John Perreault to say, "The purpose of art is spiritual, and in a word, revelation. The artist is on a quest for enlightenment or truth, engaging in the spiritual discipline of art-making. Inspiration comes only when it has been earned, and then we as viewers, if we are lucky, are able to participate in the moment of truth....the results can be transformative."

ANNENBERG'S VISION
by
Richard Roberts © 1991

The mythologist Joseph Campbell has said that the modern era depends upon artists and writers to become its mythmakers. With that thought in mind, a close scrutiny of the paintings of Maui's Andrew Annenberg reveals not only technical brilliance, but also an underlying symbolical structure of deep spiritual significance. Indeed, the term "visionary" seems appropriate when applied to this painter.

Joseph Campbell tells us in *The Hero With a Thousand Faces*,

"The adventure is always and everywhere a passage beyond the veil of the known into the unknown; the powers that watch at the boundary are dangerous.... Such demons— at once dangers and bestowers of magic powers— every hero must encounter who steps an inch outside the walls of his tradition." So too for the *artistic* adventure, and the artist/hero who ventures outside his tradition.

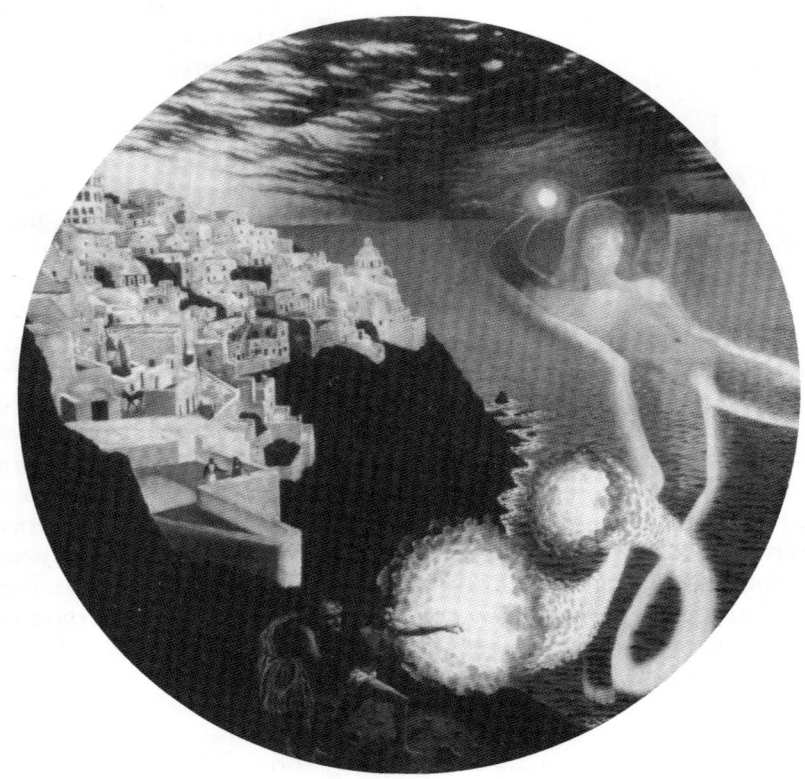

In Annenberg's "Boundless Lineage" we see at the left a middle-eastern village, the boundaries of which are sharply defined. Beyond its walls, at the edge of a cliff a youth and his teacher or master face two tunnels or vortices leading up into the sky. The master seems to be attempting to stay the headlong rush of the youth towards the tunnels, one of which leads into the vagina of a seductive, albeit celestial woman, reclining in the sky. The other tunnel or vortex circumvents the outline of her body, culminating in union with the sun. Upon closer inspection this sun appears to be the Eye of Horus of Egyptian mythology, which when presented as an offering to the mummy of Osiris, restored that deity to an eternal life. It is recalled that Horus, the son of Osiris, lost his left eye in mortal combat with the dark, antagonist principle personified by Set. The significance of the son's sacrifice in resurrecting Osiris "being susceptible to interpretation," as Joseph Campbell tells us in *The Mythic Image*, "not only in the popular sense of restoration to life following a physical death, but also, more properly, in the mystical, of an awakening to immortality through an act of psychological self-divestiture..."

In this way Annenberg's painting awakens us the viewers to the same sense of immortality which the teacher in the painting seeks to instill into the youth who seems so hell bent— shall we say— upon entering the tunnel which will lead inevitably into the womb of the celestial goddess, and thereby into further incarnations.

The parallel of Horus and Osiris to Jesus and God the Father is apparent, and brings us to Annenberg's enigmatical painting "Thou Art That". Up close it appears to be a random conglomeration of objects forming a still life set against a natural scene. However, from a distance a face manifests, the left eye of which integrates a flying pelican. Since any bird would do to form the shape of the eye, why has the painter chosen a pelican? The answer lies in the esoteric symbology of alchemy, which Jung treats in three volumes of his collected works. Before the advent of binoculars, medieval birdwatchers interpreted the sight of the pelican feeding its young from its pouch as a rending of its own breast. By this act of self-sacrifice, the pelican came to be seen as symbolic of Christ, redeeming mankind with His own blood. Again, it was the left eye of Horus which was sacrificed in order to resurrect Osiris.

In *Tarot Revelations* (1979), my collaboration with Joseph Campbell, he says that a further "understanding symbolized in the eye, the Eye of Horus" is that "one thought to be dead is disclosed to himself and to all to be in fact alive eternally, both in himself and the person of his son." Thus the son Horus is to Osiris as Christ is to God the Father. With this in mind, the meaning of Annenberg's enigmatic "Thou Art That" becomes manifest. By depicting the *left* eye as the pelican, Annenberg thereby united Horus and Christ in the sacrificial symbology linking these two paintings.

The painting's title, "Thou Art That," is derived from the Sanskrit meaning formula of the *Upanisad, tat tvam asi. Tat* denotes Brahman, the spiritual Godhead, absolute and unchangeable, *tvam*

individual man, finite and changeable; *asi* brings the two into interrelation even though by definition they are inconsistent. However, what is inconsistent between them is ultimately an illusion, for what is consistent between them is a spiritual essence, pervading the Creator's creation.

Traditional Christianity separates God and His fallen creation, but in the Buddhist and Jungian interpretations of man, there is yet within one a spiritual center, a Self or Christ awaiting redemption by the process of the Great Work to be undertaken over a lifetime. Thus, one who thinks of himself merely as dying matter may be, in Joseph Campbell's words, "disclosed to himself...to be in fact alive eternally." Annenberg's vision awakens each of us to the profound truth of the Christ within.

One word comes to mind when viewing the paintings of Andrew Annenberg. Awe. Awe in the presence of a divine, ineffable mystery. To view an Annenberg painting is to participate in that mystery.

ANNENBERG MASTERWORKS, LTD.

Andrew Annenberg's works have been collected and published worldwide. His themes recall man's earliest cultures and are universal and timeless. Andrew Annenberg's vision- expressed through his oil paintings- is boundless. The keys to Annenberg's enchanted universe are the Primal, Archetypal, Mythological or Ancient.

"Aqueous Atlantis", a stunning original, portrays the remnant of the ancient civilization of legend, now silenced by centuries beneath the sea. The aqueous ruins serve as a gathering place for the dolphins, still possessing a vibrant power, but at peace with the surrounding marine life in the ocean depths. The pillars, pyramids, and mosaic tile floor were inspired by the artist's travels, and his study of ancient Mediterranean cultures. The total vision, the expert execution in the play of underwater light, shadow and color, is typical of Annenberg's style.

Another member of the Annenberg Suite, a planned quartet of imaginative oils, is the "Portal of Hunab Ku." In Mayan mythology, Hunab Ku is the One Giver of Movement and Measure, an all-pervading conscious energy that manifests the rhythm and form in our universe. The "Portal of Hunab Ku" depicts a doorway to this ancient intelligence, a light emanating from the sea floor, with dolphins and other sea life basking in its comforting, benevolent energy.

Cibachromes are high quality reflection prints imaged directly from transparencies in a unique and exclusive manufacturing process that results in brilliant and saturated colors ensured by the use of highly pure azo dyes. This process is often used by museums for archival reproduction. Each print is hand-mounted on 1/2" Gatorfoam and coated with a High Gloss UV-Protective Film. The cibachrome is highlighted and uniqued with a minimum of three additional images painted by the artist. No two prints have the same additional images, therefore each print is unique.

The 450 Limited Editions of Lithographs are offset Lithographs with Serigraphy, which is a hand silkscreen process of laying different colors and raising certain areas texturally. The production is personally supervised by Andrew Annenberg. He creates the serigraphy screens, directs the custom mixing of premium light-fast inks, and inspects them at several stages. The screens are then destroyed so that no other identical images can be created. Paper Stock: Archival PH Neutral 100# Quintessence Gloss. All the Lithographs with Serigraphy in these Editions will be hand signed and numbered by the Artist.

If you are interested in purchasing or would like information, please contact:
Annenberg Masterworks, Ltd. P.O. Box 778, Kula, Hawaii 96790
Phone: (800) 348-3010 In Hawaii 878-3010
FAX (808) 878-1662

"Aqueous Atlantis" oil on linen 36" x 48" is available in:
Limited edition 50 unique cibachromes— Image size 36" x 48"

Limited edition 450 Lithographs with Serigraphy— Image size 24-1/2" x 33"

"Portal of Hunab Ku", oil on linen 50" x 36"
Limited edition 50 unique cibachromes— Image size 34-1/2" x 48"

Limited edition 450 Lithographs with Serigraphy— Image size 33-1/2" x 24"

"Aqueous Atlantis" and "Portal of Hunab Ku" are two

paintings of a series of four imaginative oils known as "The Annenberg Suite." The third painting in this series will be completed in the summer of 1991, with the fourth scheduled for 1992.

"Venus Triumphant" oil on linen 24 x 36"
Limited edition 50 unique cibachromes— Image size 24 x 36"

"Luminous Ascension" oil on linen 25 x 40"
Limited edition 50 unique cibachromes— Image size 25 x 40"

"Thou Art That" oil on linen 36" diameter
Limited edition 50 unique cibachromes— Image size 36" diameter

"Boundless Lineage" oil on linen 15" diameter
Limited edition 50 unique cibachromes— Image size 20" diameter

Prices for the cibachromes *start* at $3,500 to $5,500; the Lithographs begin at $800.

"Venus Triumphant"

The Chickadee Story

The day began like any other summer day in Marin County, California. I opened my curtains and stepped out on the deck. Magically, they began appearing almost at once in the two trees that overshadowed the deck, a Douglas fir, and a madrone, its red-brown bark sparkling in the sun.

Quickly I ducked back inside, returning with a handful of raw, shelled and split, redskin peanuts. Holding out my hand, the first bird dropped onto my outstretched palm, selected a peanut, and flew off to an overhead branch to peck at his treat, carefully holding the nut between his claws against the limb. Hardly had he departed than another bird dropped down to take his place. Featherlight, their touch left a slight tickling sensation in the palm.

Occasionally two would arrive at the same time to cries of indignation from both, for the pecking order had to be followed if the feeding was to proceed in an orderly manner. If, per chance, some upstart were to usurp another's place, then he might expect to be knocked sprawling from the sacred confines of my five fingers. For what was more essential to life than survival, and I was both feeding mother and father-protector to these masked birds that had endeared themselves to me by their tiny antics.

These birds were the French poodles of the aerial kingdom. I had seen them invent games to play, and when not busying themselves with feeding and drinking from the large plastic plant dish which I kept beneath their feeder, they seemed to spend much of their time sporting in the trees, often hanging upside down like swinging monkeys, and all the time chattering to one another, or to me, "chick-a-dee."

Their acrobatics enabled me to feed them from a satellite feeder, whose small opening required a tricky landing and head-dip in order to pluck from within a shelled sunflower seed, their regular staple when I was not around to hand-proffer peanuts. Their rivals for the food supply were the Oregon Juncos, or Oregon Junkies, as I referred to them, aggressive birds three times their size, who announced their arrival and bullying intents with a series of clicks, not unlike the sound a man makes to gee-up his horse. They could empty a feeder in minutes, as could the screeching jays that filled a craw and bill with an ordinary bird's daily ration, and then flew off to deposit it in a tree trunk until the overstuffed jay was ready to feed again.

As I watched the feeding, a holding pattern began to develop over my head, as those who had finished their treats waited for the next available moment to alight. After a time, my arm began to tire, but spotting Shadow I raised my hand to within a foot of his limb. Still he had not eaten, and I would never be satisfied until he had taken a seed or nut from my hand.

Shadow was two, perhaps three years old. Even the youngsters born this year had mustered enough courage to land on the awesome hand; yet Shadow remained alone and afraid. He came by his name legitimately. When he would flutter down to land or to drink, his shadow suddenly appearing before him would frighten him off, and he would retreat with the chickadee alarm cry, a high-pitched single note that I took to mean "help!"

By contrast, Whitey, the flock's brave leader, was so accustomed to me that if he saw me through the window sitting in my writing-chair, he would fly to the door's handle and perch, or hang upside down from the gable, peering in at me with his bright, beady eyes. Then I could not resist, and would grab a few nuts, open the door, and thrust out my hand, on which he landed immediately. Once, in a moment which assured me of his complete confidence in me, instead of flying off to eat his nut, he began to peck away at it while still within my open palm. His mate was always with him and would fly down for a nut moments after him. Indeed, these two were the pioneers who taught the whole flock their bravery, for only after watching their performance for many days did the other birds begin to follow suit. Except, of course, for Shadow.

While all the other birds were hammering away at the peanuts with their beaks like a flock of rapid-drill woodpeckers, poor little Shadow would flit from limb to limb just above my hand. If my hand followed him to beneath his limb, he would peer anxiously over his shoulder and hop away again, always with his cry for help. I had heard birds from other flocks use this signal to warn others when startled or surprised, but in Shadow's case his own flock must have felt that he was crying wolf too often, for they never looked up from their feeding as he fled each time from my following hand. After awhile he would sit on a limb high enough above my hand where he knew there could be no danger, and he would turn his back on me and sulk at not getting a nut. Of course, if I were to throw a nut on the deck, he would fly down for it, except if another bird went for it at the same moment, whereupon he would break off his flight with a loud scream, "Help!" But I was trying to help him grow up, and so would not give in. What he fed on, I did not know, but he was not emaciated, so I'm sure he got enough of the flock's more natural food. Indeed, the others must have been so stuffed on nuts and seeds that he probably got all their bugs.

My life at this time was very solitary, in a remote, heavily forested area of Marin with hundreds of acres to use for walking and biking. In effect, these birds were my only companions, a writer's life being a solitary craft. Having neither dog nor cat, these birds were my wild pets; hence, I spared no expense to spoil them and keep them around. My worst fear was that they might migrate. In previous years, they had come to my deck for water, but never had taken seeds, even when left on the rim of the water dish, and they had disappeared for three or four months in each of those years, migrating down the coast to warmer weather no doubt.

I hoped that when they were there that they stayed with another lonely writer, perhaps in Santa Barbara, who could feed them as well as I. Recently I had begun to hand-proffer tamari-coated cashews for their morning treat. Since these had more flavor than the raw peanuts, I imagined their taste buds were dancing on their tiny tongues.

The more I watched them, the more I came to know and name each one. The personality differences were subtle, but when one is observing a bird as close as one's hand, then even the expression in the eyes can be observed. Only a dozen birds comprised the flock, and the species was somewhat special. The Black-capped Chickadee ranges over most of the northern U.S. and Canada, summering in a large part of Alaska. Then there is a Carolina Chickadee which ranges from Texas to about New Jersey. And two more varieties, the Mountain and Mexican Chickadees make their homes in the mountain heights from northern Canada to southern Mexico, the latter indigenous only to Mexico.

My variety was the Chestnut-Backed Chickadee, distinguished from all others by the reddish brown coloring on its back. Their range was from Alaska to southern California along a narrow strip of the Pacific Coast, where they could avoid the freezing temperatures of the mountainous areas inland. All chickadees have black bibs and white cheeks, topped by black caps that run around the sides masking the eyes, but in Whitey's case his head was practically all white. I wondered whether old age or wisdom had turned his head white.

In the summer, while sunbathing on the deck, I would lie down with a tray of seeds and nuts beside me, the air around me filled with the beating of their wings. On these hot days, water was even more important to them than food, and I kept a three inch deep, plastic dish clean and full. Each individual style of bathing again revealed their personality differences, and gave me many hours of entertainment.

Some took a no-nonsense attitude to the bath, plunging in without further ado, and then hopping out and drying off as fast as possible. Others couldn't stay out of the water, just like kids at the seaside. But some, particularly the young ones, seemed to fear the depths and would get in by degrees, dipping a wing here, or a tail there before finally immersing themselves. Shadow, of course, was the most afraid. He would flutter around the edge, splashing some water on himself, while holding onto the side with one claw, hollering all the time.

Naturally I fed other birds with a wild birdseed, which the Dees never touched. One day the Dee's ingenuity topped all that I had seen before. The hummingbird feeder had a long glass tube on one end, which continually filled as the birds drank by inserting their tongues into the end. If the Dees were nearby, they would hang upside down from the roof rafters and carefully watch the hummingbirds, trying to figure out how to drink like them. However, since their tongues were not long enough, they could not get any of the very sweet water in the hummingbird feeder. They would imitate the hummingbirds and hang at the tip of the feeder, but all in vain. Then one day while one was hanging on the end, another landed on the top of the feeder, causing it to sway, and spilling nectar from the end, which that bird drank up. The pair would then change positions, rocking the feeder back and forth, enabling the other bird to drink. Soon many of the Dees were doing this, and I had trouble keeping the feeder full. Shadow, however, stuck to his bug and water diet.

By now I could whistle them up. Two or three loud whistles in imitation of their song, and one or two birds would appear almost at once, swiftly followed by the rest of the flock. My biggest kick came from "Chickadee Football." Setting a nearly round peanut on the deck, I would watch the first bird try to pick it up in its beak. Being too large, it would roll a little ways, whereupon another bird would peck at it, rolling it again. Back and forth it would move, one way and another, as many birds tried to claim it for their own.

There were other birds around, of course, including a wise Great Horned owl who was always asking "Who, who?", but I never knew the answer to his question. None of the other birds, however, gave me as much delight as my chickadees, so I shall share with you the story of their journey.

All of the flock was feeling it, and asking Whitey when they would be leaving. But Whitey was aware that never before had it been so good. He wouldn't hesitate to leave if the supply of peanuts, sunflower seeds, and tamari-covered cashews ran out, and so he was the first to come to the deck each morning to see if food was still available. As to the red soda pop the youngsters got from the hummingbird's tube, well, that was a little too sweet for his mature tastes, so he could do without that. Water wasn't the problem. Their migratory route was always near enough to the sea so that fog droplets on a leaf would quench a thirst. But there had been some lean years before—few seeds and insects—and some of the flock had been too weak to return. No, Whitey felt, they were better off where they were. Besides, he had fun making the man come to the door with a handful of food. He liked the man, and would miss him if they went away.

But the urge to migrate became a kind of rebellion in his flock, so Whitey decided to hold a parliament of birds to put it to the vote if necessary. Each Dee had a say, and although Whitey's words made sense, most of the flock said, "My instinct tells me we must be on our way." When all was said and done, it was decided that they would leave next day at the very crack of dawn, breakfasting on sunflower seeds from the feeder before the man in the big house was yet awake.

After their decision was made, Whitey flew to the deck and peered in the window at the man, whose back was turned to him. He appeared not to notice Whitey as he pushed a stick-like object back and forth across a white expanse on which marks materialized under the stick.

Well, thought Whitey, this would be the last chance to say goodbye. They would be gone long before the man's curtains opened in the morning. Whitey thought of the man's funny whistle when he called them up to the deck for breakfast. He could never get the notes quite right. A Dee-dee always sounded like a Dee-dee, but the man's whistle always sounded different each time, and never was on key. Why couldn't humans whistle? It was the easiest and most natural thing in the world, and yet they couldn't get it right.

Whitey decided it was because birds were smarter than people, although he was amazed at the size of the nest where the man lived. It was made of wood and solid air. The man had marked the solid air with brightly colored spots so that the flock would not run into it and get hurt. One time a peregrine falcon had swooped down on the deck and had broken its neck when stopped by the solid air. Sometimes the man moved the solid air aside and made it soft again when he came outside to feed the flock, or to lie in the sun.

Another time Whitey had followed the man back inside and had to be rescued by the man, because most of the nest inside was solid

152

air, and Whitey kept banging his head as he flew from one end of the nest to the other. Stunned, the man had come and gently lifted him down from a ledge. He set Whitey outside in the shade, and after a while Whitey was able to fly away. He decided never to go into the man's nest again.

Whitey fluttered down to the handle on the solid air, the one the man used to move it aside. Tapping twice with his beak, he saw the man turn and smile at him.

"Okay, I'm coming, Whitey," said the man. He slid open the glass door and dipped his hand into a bowl of peanuts and sunflower seeds. Whitey flew into the outstretched palm, but instead of taking a nut and flying off, he just sat still looking into the man's face. "What's wrong, old pal, not hungry today?"

The bird continued to gaze at the man, who now brought his palm closer to his face. Whitey looked downcast into the pile of nuts and sunflower seeds all around his feet. Reaching up to his palm with his other hand, the man picked up a sunflower seed and moved it towards Whitey's beak. With a last long look into the man's eyes, the bird flew off.

"Oh, well," thought Whitey, "you could never make humans understand anyhow."

The man put the handful of food into the feeder and went back to his writing.

The next day dawned warm and beautiful with a delicate fog hugging the coast like a white nightgown. Some of the youngsters had slept restlessly, for anticipation of what was to be their first migration had kept them awake much of the night. Beyond flying three or four miles around White's Hill, they had never been away from home.

Soon they were all flying in a loose chickadee formation behind Whitey and Garlinda his mate. When they reached the wide expanse of water known as the Golden Gate, between Marin and San Francisco, a strong breeze sprang up from the northwest to help push them across. They took some water and seeds from a feeder near the Cliff House, and watched the tourists watching the waves break on Seal Rocks. "Humans have such simple pleasures," thought Whitey. And he recalled again the man in Marin who spent hours motionless in his solid air nest, except for the stick which he moved over and over again across the white expanse in his lap.

Then they were flying again. Around Mt. San Bruno they saw and heard the giant roaring birds that constantly landed and rose again from one great place on the ground. Whitey had taken them quite close to that spot one year, but they found no food and only hard, hard ground that hurt their beaks, so Whitey stuck closer to the ocean this time. What the giant birds had found there to eat, Whitey could not imagine.

By midday they were at the end of the reservoir, where they found many insects along the banks. Splashing about, the youngsters played in the shallow waters, and there was time for everyone to have a bath. Even Shadow managed to duck his head in the water for a moment, but the sudden rush of cold water over his eyes made him cry for help three times. Whitey was thinking that perhaps they were right to want to leave. Roughing it wasn't so bad after all.

Near dark they were in the foothills of the Santa Cruz mountains, and there they spent the night.

The next morning the fog had pushed inland during the night, wetting their feathers and dousing their spirits considerably. The first reaction of each was to fly up to the man's deck for a hearty breakfast of peanuts and tamari cashews, but there was no deck to fly to, and all directions seemed uncertain in the shroud-like fog. Whitey had an uneasy foreboding about the day, but as their leader he knew better than to convey it to the flock. And so he gave a string of commands about keeping a tight flying formation, and the importance of periodically sounding the chickadee rallying cry so that a bird who had lost visual contact could regain the formation. Whitey knew to keep the northwest wind pushing at his tail feathers in order to fly along the path of their southeasterly migration. They fed sporadically during that day, and only in late afternoon did the fog lift, revealing scattered houses beneath them. The youngsters were complaining about how tired and hungry they were, so Whitey decided to explore the backyards of the houses for feeders.

Presently they came to a house with a large patio at the back and more feeders than they had ever seen before. In the air was the smell of peanut butter, and there were gobs of it stuck under the middle of boxes propped up by sticks. A beautiful woman was lying on the patio sleeping in the sun. When the chickadees landed in her trees and began a few tentative calls to announce themselves, she awoke and began to talk to them. "Pretty birds, come and get the nice peanut butter. Momma's got a *big* surprise for you."

Little did they know, the feeders were all traps which could be collapsed over the birds by pulling on strings. For the lady owned a pet shop in Santa Cruz, and she sold chickadees in cages to her customers.

The youngsters were anxious to get at the peanut butter, but held back in deference to Whitey's priority as number one. He looked at the woman, and wondered why she did not try to whistle like a Dee as the man in Marin had done. Something bothered him about the way her eyes gleamed, but the smell of peanut butter became more and more overpowering, and the youngsters hopped eagerly from limb to limb and cried out at him to get on with it.

"If you don't want to eat, we will!" "We're hungry," they whined. "Get out of the way."

Whitey was just about to make his move when he heard a Dee calling from within the house. The warning came just in time; for he had started to fly under the box, veering off at the last moment just as the woman jerked one of her strings. The box slammed down, almost catching Whitey's wingtip. "Help!" screamed Shadow. And all at once they were all chirping "help!" and following Whitey, who had swerved past the woman's head and out over the patio away from the house. The sudden deception of a human had so unnerved Whitey and the rest of the flock that they kept in the air until nearly dark. When they landed, there was not enough light left to search for food. Huddling in a hole in an old rotten log, they comforted themselves as best they could.

The next morning they awoke to raucous cries that commenced before dawn and grew louder as the morning lightened. The sounds were the bird equivalent of laughter, and seemed to surround them in the forest. Whitey roused himself from a guarded sleep and flew off to investigate. A few hundred yards away a group of jays and crows marched around on a mountain meadow, squawking back and forth. They seemed to be telling bird jokes in which a jay or crow always outdid or outsmarted a bird of another species. And at each punchline, they all joined in with raucous cawing.

Whitey decided that they seemed harmless enough, and went back for the rest of the flock, but when they landed in the meadow with the crows, their reception was anything but friendly.

"Where are you birds from?" said the ringleader, a disheveled old crow who had an old cigarette butt stuck in his beak. He wore a small cap pulled down over one eye.

"We're from north of San Francisco," said Whitey, trying to impress them, since they behaved like big-city birds.

"We don't want no Frisco birds here," said the bird, whose name was Chauncey.

"Well, actually it's not Frisco," said Whitey, "but Marin County."

His disclaimer started all the birds laughing. A particularly presumptuous jay, who was Chauncey's sidekick, bellied up to

Whitey. "No more grubs for me, mater, I'm off to Marin to have buttered scones and tea!"

All the jays and crows fell to the ground at that moment and rolled around in a fit of laughter, flapping their wings feebly.

Whitey was rapidly losing face in light of this avian repartee, and did not know what to say. Garlinda, his mate, decided to speak.

"We're all hungry, and wondered if you could direct us to where we might find something to eat."

Eyeing her, the leader replied, "Well, what is it you birds eat?"

"Peanuts," said Garlinda. "Peanuts!" said Chauncey. "That's human food. We can't get you no peanuts."

"Well, perhaps sunflower seeds without the shells. Our little ones find it so hard to get at the meat that they need the shells opened."

Jethro, Chauncey's sidekick jay, waddled over to Garlinda and bowed low before her. "Would you like us to open up a dozen ersters for you, Mi'lady." Now the crows and jays were holding up one another with their wings to keep from falling down because they were laughing so hard. Whitey's patience was wearing thin. He felt like giving Jethro a punch up the beak.

When the cawing had subsided, Chauncey said, "Any other requests?"

Some of the youngsters piped up. "Cashews with tamari sauce." This brought the house down again. Some of the jays and crows were so weak from laughing that they could no longer stand, but flapped weakly around on the ground.

"We ought to keep you birds around for laughs," said Chauncey.

Jethro strutted up to Whitey. "Hey, you, the old guy with all the snow on the roof. You'll be givin' me crows' feet from laughin'."

"We call 'em jays' feet," said Chauncey, correcting him.

"You must be the leader of this bunch," said Jethro. Whitey nodded, standing as tall as he could. "Well, how come you don't know where to lead your birds to find food? Huh? That's your job, ain't it?" said Jethro.

"Aw, leave 'em alone," said Chauncey. "They're lost. C'mon, I'll show you our stash." Flapping his wings, Chauncey lifted into the air, followed by all the other birds. They had not gone very far when they came to what appeared to be a mound of different-colored rocks and pebbles piled just inside the mouth of a cave.

"Here's what we eat," said Chauncey proudly. "Help yourself."

"What is it?" said all the Dees, crowding around. "Birds' eggs, stolen from their nests!" said Jethro proudly. "Here's a gull's egg, and some robins', and there's even some chickadee eggs," he said, pointing with his wing.

One of the young Dees spoke up. "These are all babies who will never be born."

"You're right there, Junior," said Jethro. "And that means more for us."

Another young Dee named Henrietta quietly asked her mother, "Why won't they be born, mother?"

"Because they need their mother's warmth to hatch them."

Young Henrietta's maternal instincts got the better of her, and she hopped up on the mound of eggs and sat on the topmost one, spreading her wings down the side in order to allow her body heat to radiate downward.

"Come down from there, Henrietta. Those eggs have been dead for months."

"What is dead?" said all the youngsters at once, suddenly frightened.

"Do you mean all the birds in that pile of eggs can never come out, never see the sun, never feel the sky under their wings?"

"Never taste a peanut?" "Never float on the wind?" Each of the young Dees had a different question to ask about the meaning of dead, and each was unanswerable.

Chauncey: "You birds need to educate them kids in the basic facts of life. How come they don't know what dead is? Every crow and jay does."

Whitey: "Because you take life by eating other's eggs. We chickadees respect life."

Jethro, starting to strut: "We'll show you what dead is," he said, pointing at a crow with his wingtip.

Crow: "Pushing up daisies!" Jethro, pointing at a jay.

Jay: "Gone West!"

Crow: "With the eyes crossed out! Like this." With an elaborate, Hollywood-type death, he staggers around and around in circles. "You got me! I'm cashing in my chips." Falling down he pulls out a pencil and marks crosses on his eyelids.

Shadow, not wishing to see anymore of their display, flies off a little ways, and pointedly turns his back, looking this way and that, as if some pressing matter had called him.

Jethro: "What's wrong with him? Can't he take it?"

Shadow's mother: "He's sensitive, that's all."

Chauncey: "Aw, we was only havin' a little fun. No need for him to get touchy."

Whitey: "Sometimes things scare him that don't scare others, but that doesn't make him any less scared."

Jethro: "Well, we ain't gonna hurt him."

Whitey: "Shadow! Come up here next to me. We were all in on the decision to migrate, and we must all help one another now."

Reluctantly, and fidgeting on his limb, Shadow finally flew up.

Shadow: "Well, I didn't want to leave home."

Whitey: "The question is what do we do now that we are here. Fretting won't help."

Chauncey, strutting up to Whitey and Shadow: "I'll tell you birds what you might do. Only yesterday we was in a field where a farmer had just cut the crop. There was lots of seeds and little teeny bugs and stuff like youse birds like to eat."

All the chickadees gathered around him demanding to know where this field could be found.

Chauncey: "If youse wants, I'll give you directions. Head south towards the sun about five miles. When you come to the freeway—you can't miss it—hang a right and follow it down out of the mountains. Just before you come into town, you'll see the farmer's field on your left. You'll know it by the—pardon the expression—scarecrow, a crude replica of a human which wouldn't even scare your friend Shadow there."

Soon they were airborne again. Whitey had insisted that Shadow stay just behind him in their formation, and now Shadow was thinking how easy it was to fly with another breaking the wind ahead of him. There was time to look around and take joy in the cloud shapes unfurling around him, and in the highway unwinding below.

Garlinda was proudest at Whitey's side, for she had always known that he was the wisest and most beautiful of birds. During their courtship, he had lined their tree-hole nest with the softest of mosses and lichens, softer even than the fuzzy covering of the floor of the nest of the peanut-man. And sometimes, when Whitey had eaten his fill and the peanut-man still held out his hand to them, Whitey would fly off with the nut to their nest, there to hide it where she would find it when snuggling down for the night's rest. Then Whitey would act nonchalantly, as if to say, "Fancy finding that there."

Garlinda watched with pride the effortless way that Whitey banked to turn to follow the road below. For a while, until they found the road, she was not sure whether or not the crows were playing a trick. She was glad they had not deceived Whitey, for she loved him so much that she hated to see him lose face in the eyes of the other birds. Turning her head slightly, she saw Shadow behind Whitey to

158

her left. This was the first time in his life he had done anything but bring up the rear, and he seemed to be enjoying himself immensely. Garlinda hoped that this spring she would bear Whitey a son. All the previous years her eggs had not hatched or had been eaten by other birds. She had seen the peanut-man shoot one of the murdering jays, and when it tumbled out of the tree, squawking once and lying lifeless, she felt no pity, only remorse that it had not happened sooner, before her son-to-be had been destroyed.

Shadow saw Garlinda turn to look at him and for a moment wanted to fold his wings and hide at the back of the flock, but from the smile in her eye he knew she was glad he was there, and gladdened himself, he ventured closer to Whitey's tailfeathers.

Further back in the flock, Shadow's mother, puffed-up with pride, caught the eye of Shadow's father, and the two of them thought as one, "Maybe he will turn out all right after all."

An hour or so before dark, Whitey led them in a long glide into the farmer's field. They buzzed the old straw hat atop the scarecrow and settled down to a serious chow-down, for this was the first good feed since the marsh site two days before. With the December darkness falling rapidly, Whitey wanted to find a safe haven for the night, and so, while the others still fed, and with his stomach only half-full, he flew off with Garlinda at his side. There was an old barn only a half mile away in which the loft door had fallen off. Inside there was plenty of warm hay and straw to shelter the flock for the night.

The next day, at first light, Whitey surveyed the scene before him. They were near the ocean. A salt breeze filled his beak, and ahead an early morning fog clung to the edge of the land like down to the breast of a newly hatched chick. Towards the ocean was a treeless expanse of cultivated fields, dissected by a network of narrow roads. Although food would be easy to spot in such places, Whitey also knew there was greater danger without the cover of trees to hide them. No, they would not go that way. Towards the southeast, distant mountains promised the woodlands he sought.

It was well after midday that the uplands began to rise under their tiring wings. Thirst was making their tongues brittle. Each remembered vividly now the cool, clean expanse of water on the peanut-man's deck. When they closed their eyes, they could see it sparkling in the sun. It was then, after drinking, that they would flap into that liquid delight for the morning bath. Shadow, too, thought of that water. "If I could be there now," he said to the wind, "I'd put my whole head underwater. Honest, I would." The wind did not listen and soared on by. "What is this instinct," thought Shadow, "that makes us leave what is good to fly to places we know not?"

For the second day, Shadow was flying behind Whitey. The small scrubby bushes gave way to gnarled, white live oaks, broad-branched firs and conical green pines, and eventually to giant redwoods that tickled the bellies of passing clouds.

At such times as this, with the flock skimming in, out, and around the tips of redwoods at breakneck speed, swaying in the wind, to be a bird was the best of all things in life.

Sometime later they had found a mountain creek, where they all had a long, long drink, although its babbling scared Shadow, and he gave many a cry for help before finding a pool quiet enough to let him drink. Nearby was a path, strewn with human drinking cans, and discarded food boxes floated in endless circles in the stream's pools. From the path there came the sound of whistling. All at once, the memory of the peanut-man came flooding back to the flock. They could see once more the open hand and the red skins of the peanuts glistening in the morning sun, smell the ripe odor of the nut oils wafting on the wind, and taste finally on their tongues the tang of temptation. Whitey was the first there, the others arranging themselves in the branches above the human's head.

It was not the peanut-man, but perhaps Whitey thought, he had something to offer. The boy looked up at the same moment Whitey started down. The stone struck Whitey in the breast, breaking his neck. He fell in a long crazy spiral to the feet of the boy. "Stupid bird," he said, not even bothering to inspect his victim.

Shadow had screamed "help!" and broken away. Garlinda was so close to Whitey that the stone carried on to break her wing. Painfully, she clung to the twig on the tree above Whitey's body. When the boy had passed, she released her grip and tumbled down on top of Whitey, breaking her wing still further. The rest of the flock flew down to Whitey, except for Shadow who had turned his back on the pandemonium and hoped above hope that it would all go away. He knew he must be having a nightmare. He would awaken; it would be morning; Whitey would be there to lead them.

Garlinda bent her head to Whitey's breast, but his heart had stopped beating the moment the stone had wrenched his neck halfway around his body. Only one eye was visible, and had glazed and closed, the other lay under his head, half-buried in mud. They were all terribly frightened. The world had closed down on them like a huge trap. All of them were thinking, "This is what dead is." But for Garlinda, whose life had always been at Whitey's side, the light that had been Whitey, that danced always for her in his eye, had gone out, and with it had gone Whitey, she knew not where. She asked them with her eyes, where had Whitey gone? Ashamed at their helplessness, they turned away from her eyes.

Later as they clung perilously to the branches overhead, they heard her cry out just once, and then the world had such a silence that it hurt their sleep through the rest of that longest night.

Hours before morning the wind shifted strongly to the east, and with it blew a chill tulle fog from the valley. As if their spirits were not dampened enough, this fog condensed its frosty breath on their eyes and beaks, feathers and claws, and turned the branches on which they perched into icy fingers, which corpse-like beckoned them to their death.

At the spot where Whitey had fallen, nothing remained except a few drops of blood. The rat had done his work well.

As the fog thickened and lightened with the passing of the wind, the world came and went, disappearing and then manifesting like shapes of a nightmare.

Shadow thought to himself, there can be no bird in all the world more miserable than I am. Would that the rat had got me too.

And it was, at that moment of his greatest misery, that there appeared alongside him in the undergrowth, another chickadee, not a Chestnut-Back like himself, but a Black-Cap, blown some fifty miles away from her flock and lost for more than a week. She greeted Shadow with chickadee song, but miserable as he was, he wondered how anyone could look to him for anything at all.

"I'm lost too," was all Shadow could reply.

The world remained ghostly for the rest of that morning, trees appearing and disappearing as the fog cloaked them. They could not fly, and there was nothing on the ground to eat. The cold creek water alone sustained them.

The stray chickadee from the valley stayed close to Shadow, for all of the other birds in the flock appeared to be mated. He wondered if she could possibly know how scared he was. No, she wouldn't be following me if she knew. I'll have to try to be a little braver, he resolved.

Towards midday the fog began to lighten somewhat, and they found an enclosed bower in which sunflower seeds had been stashed by a bird or animal. Unlike those given them by the peanut-man, these seeds still bore their hard jackets, which the Dees could split only by persistent pecking, and even then not all would yield their sweet inner meat.

The youngsters fretted, "Why would anyone want to put the seed in a tough old skin like this? No one can eat it!"

"Junior," said the mothers, "that's the way the seeds were born."

"Well then," they asked, "did the peanut-man take the shells off for us?"

"That's right, junior. So that you wouldn't knock your brains out trying to get breakfast."

"Why can't we have a peanut-man all the time, wherever we go?"

"You'd have to ask your father that. I'm sure I don't know."

By now, the flock had been feeding for half an hour and the sky was becoming quite bright. The stray asked Shadow why he did not go into the bower for breakfast. "Because I'm not hungry," he sulked. Leaving him, she entered the narrow mouth at the bottom of the bower. Shadow turned around on his branch and pretended not to be interested in breakfast. From time to time quick, flitting shadows passed overhead, unseen by the other birds in the enclosed bower. Suddenly a shadow materialized and alighted at the mouth of the bower. It was a red-tail hawk, eyes glistening at the sight of an entire flock of small birds trapped with no way out except by the entry way guarded by his terrible talons. Some of the Dees froze, too petrified by fear to stir even a feather. The youngsters fluttered from side to side, smashing into one another. Content with his complete mastery, the hawk waited and savored the moment.

It was in this moment of hesitation that something struck him in the head, knocking him off balance. Before he could regain his equilibrium, he was hit again, then again. Staggering into the air, he made off without ever seeing that the small bird that had driven him off, that had saved the flock, was none other than Shadow.

The next day a great change had come over the flock. Leaderless, they had been many. Now by mutual consent with Shadow to lead them, they became one. For Shadow, although he accepted his new role humbly, the only problem was where to lead them. In most ways, he was the same Shadow he had been before attacking the hawk. His act was not so much courage as instinct. Had he time to reflect before acting, undoubtedly he would have flown away. But something compelled him even more than his desire to save the flock, and that was his growing attachment for the stray, whose name was Devalinda.

In her eyes, Shadow had always been a hero. In her imagining, he fulfilled her expectation of the chosen one. As far as she knew, behind him unfurled a legend of great deeds, all pointing toward the one moment culminating in the act that would win her heart. As for the rest of the flock, they were so startled by Shadow's uncharacteristic valor that it was as if a new bird had been born in that moment to lead

162

them; hence, the past slate was wiped clean, never to be mentioned again.

And so in the eyes of all the birds, Shadow was a reborn hero, assuming the role of the mighty leader Whitey before him. But Shadow was still Shadow; only now he knew the role he was supposed to play, and— more importantly— *how* to live up to it. This made him a hero.

Still he wasn't any wiser for being the braver, and, therefore, hadn't the foggiest idea of how to get them home. For they were all agreed upon returning now. Instinct had had its day, and the urge to migrate had run its course. Devalinda was accepted into the flock because Shadow accepted her. None would question his judgment. When he told her of redskin peanuts and tamari-covered cashews she could only blink, believing such things to be part and parcel of the myth of manna from heaven.

Shadow wisely sent out scouting parties to inquire of all the woodland creatures as to the way home. Of course, to each one, the word "home" meant something quite different. To the serpent, a certain hole in the ground served that purpose. And, so, in the end, they were right back where they had started from, until a skunk, queried by Shadow himself, told them to ask the Oracle. Who or what was the Oracle the skunk did not know, but at the dark of the moon it was certain to appear, sitting in a tree just above the bower. Since that night was the very time described by the skunk, they gathered round and waited for night to fall.

The youngsters had dozed off, and Devalinda was snuggled under Shadow's wing, when an eerie cry called down to them, and two ghostly eyes gleamed in the dark. "Who, who?" it said.

Trying to sound like a leader, if not feeling like one in the face of such a challenge, Shadow replied, "We are just a flock of chickadees, lost while migrating. We ask your Excellency, your Highness, for his wise counsel in finding our way home."

"Where, where?" came the reply. "Oh, home for us is Marin County beyond the Golden Gate."

"How, how?"

"How came we here? South, south, across the Golden Gate."

"Tomorrow, tomorrow," said the Oracle, "when the sun first rises you must fly away towards the west until you reach the sea. Then fly with the sun at your back north, until you come to the Golden Gate. When you cross it you will be in Marin once more."

"Of course," said Shadow, "how simple. Why didn't I think of that?"

"You will, you will," said the Oracle.

"We thank your Almightyness for helping us to find our way again."

"Is there anything else you wish to know? I have the answers to everything."

"No, no, we thank you kindly...."

Just then, one of the youngsters interrupted, his small, piping voice carrying over the trees, into the sky, and out beyond to the stars, where it reverberated back to earth.

"Dead, dead," it said, "what is the meaning of dead?"

The two golden eyes of the Oracle blinked for a moment and went out. Then its voice answered once more.

"Who, who?" it said. "Who perishes does but renew and vary his form."

There was silence in the flock. Their thoughts were on Whitey and Garlinda. It was as if they were there in the trees with them. Shadow could feel Whitey's presence in his wings; a new strength surged through him.

Morning found them flying away from the sun towards the ocean, following the Oracle's wise counsel. The flock's flying formation was the same as when they had departed from Marin, except that now Shadow and Devalinda led the way.

The day was sparkling clear with hardly a breath of wind. Looking east over her shoulder, Devalinda saw the snow-clad peaks of the Sierras, and the forested foothills from where she had flown. She wondered about the magic land of Marin to which they were returning, and why, if it were as wonderful as they all said, they had left it in the first place.

They had not flown more than three hours, when far below the great sea breakers unfurled their crested plumes. They were all chattering to themselves. Shadow knew that some of them had doubts about his abilities to lead them, but the seacoast was a welcome sight, reassuring them that all would be well. Shadow led them in a slow majestic turn to the north that incorporated a shallow dive. Now that they had found the way, they could fly lower to the ground, alert to whatever feeding opportunities might arise.

At mid-afternoon, Shadow spotted a golden, undulating serpent far off to the right, which pointed inevitably towards the Golden Gate, for it was the water of the very reservoir to which Whitey had taken them, now reflecting the golden light of the sinking sun. As Shadow brought them in for a landing, he could read in their eyes the new pride they felt in him. There were insects and grubs galore for all to eat. As Shadow sat on a limb, cleaning his bill by rubbing it side to side on the limb, he thought, "This is the very spot on which I perched just a few days ago. But what a different bird I am now! If anyone had said, 'You shall lead the flock back,' I would have replied, 'I could not do it. What a funny thing is life.'

Devalinda joined him and cleaned her bill just as he had done. Then all the flock followed suit. Devalinda gently touched her bill against Shadow's. And best of all, thought Shadow, now I have a mate.

The birds had been gone from my deck for almost a week now. In the satellite feeder, the sunflower seeds languished, and the ten pound bag of peanuts sat disconsolately in the corner, its contents growing stale. Each day I had been eating a little more of the tamari-covered cashews. Without my birds to talk with, I spent more time watching television, or on the telephone with friends I had not called in months. And, of course, my writing fell off.

Migration, I supposed, was inevitable no matter how well I fed my chickadees. I wondered if another flock migrating from the north might stumble upon my deck on the way, and perhaps decide to stay. That was just wishful thinking.

I had risen late that morning and was seated at the breakfast table with the sliding glass door to the deck ajar when I heard the unmistakable cry, "Chick-a-dee-dee." It gladdened my heart. I jumped up and went out on the deck to hear better. Suddenly I saw the first bird, then the others closely behind.

Thinking these birds not tame enough to feed from my hand, I dumped a pile of seeds into an open bowl and set it on the railing. Not a bird made a move towards the seeds, nor towards the satellite. Some dropped down for water, then flew up to the madrone branches just inches over my head. Then suddenly it dawned on me. These were my birds! Shadow was the closest to me, but where was Whitey?

Grabbing a handful of shelled peanuts, I stuck my open palm up towards Shadow, fully expecting him to fly away. Instead, he hopped down into my hand, looked me right in the eye, and began pecking at a nut. Moments later, another bird joined him. This bird did not have the rufous-red back borne by all the flock.

"You sly devil," I said to Shadow, "you've come back with a mate."

All the flock was anxious to feed, but they dared not transgress the pecking order as long as Shadow and Devalinda sat in the peanut-man's hand. Their trip that day across the Golden Gate had been an easy one, and a straight line north from Mt. Tam had brought them home. Finally Shadow relented and took his nut to an overhead twig. Shadow showed her how to wrap her claw around the nut and the limb in order to keep the nut from slipping out, but she flubbed it the first time and her peanut rattled to the deck, where it was scooped up by one of the youngsters. The pecking order applied to the sequence of feeding so that everything went off like clockwork, but once you dropped your food, it became fair game for anyone.

Shadow flew back into the peanut-man's hand to get another nut for Devalinda. The man was amused by the change in Shadow, and said to him, "How come you're not a scaredy-cat anymore?"

Shadow looked him right in the eye and thought, "Well, when you've dealt with hawks, humans aren't that scary."

All the flock tittered at that, and hopped from limb to limb applauding Shadow.

Before long, the peanut-man came out with three large feeding dishes, one of peanuts, another of sunflower seeds, and a third of cashews, coated with the most marvelous flavor that Devalinda had ever tasted. She was sure she would never eat another worm again!

She had been afraid that the flock had been telling her tall tales about the treats the peanut-man prepared for them, but this feeding exceeded her wildest dreams. She wondered, as she surveyed the sequence of the various foods in the three dishes, if this was what humans meant by "buffet."

Meanwhile, the youngsters, after eating their fill, had climbed up on the hummingbird feeder and were taking turns drinking from the opening while the others rocked it back and forth. After a while they got a sugar high from the strawberry "pop," as they called it, and kept rocking it just for the fun of it, all the while chattering a little song that they had made up for the occasion.

"Yo, ho, ho and a bottle of pop, we're gonna rock 'til our folks say 'stop.'"

But no one wanted to stop their fun. Their parents just sat in the trees and watched. No one had even bothered to fly home to the nests, even though they were right around the corner. The peanut-man had been working inside, in between keeping the trays full, and now he came out carrying a paper banner which he hung on a string in the lower branches just above the feeding trays. The words on it said, "WELCOME HOME, CHICKADEES."

As the months passed, this flock came to know the meaning of freedom, for it was decided unanimously that they would never give in to mere instinct again. They would never act again like other birds, but with a freedom to choose to migrate or to stay, they would stay

166

here for the rest of their lives as long as the peanut-man could provide for them.

Shadow, as he matured, became something of a philosopher. He referred to the life of other species of birds as "a grubby existence," and was given to reminding the flock from time to time that "this is really living." None could disagree with him.

My joy at the return of my Dees was lessened by the realization that Whitey and his mate would not return. At first I had thought that he might have sent the flock on ahead while he made a detour, the importance of which only he knew. What events had caused him to leave the flock I could not imagine, but I feared the worst. I saw myself in Whitey, the adventurer who was the first to trust a human, the dare-devil who could take a seed from a hand. Somehow my own trust in humans lessened with each day that Whitey did not return.

And thoughts of his mortality began to arouse within me the dread of my own death, for lucky, indeed, is the man who can say, this is the one place on earth where he loves to be, but then, his thoughts become fixed on his earthly Paradise and he fears that which might take him away from it.

But these were winter thoughts, and as the spring came on, the madrones were transformed into maidens clad in white garlands which showered the deck, and the air was so heady with fragrance that spring was like a beautiful woman who had come to live in my house.

Gradually, when they could fly, the new spring chicks were brought to the deck. Unlike other birds, these chicks seemingly wanted to feed themselves, almost from the first day. Unlike the Juncoes and Finches whose young kept demanding to be fed months after it was necessary, the tiny Dees were very independent.

One day there was a great stir among the flock, an annunciation of twittering, as it were, and I saw that Shadow and his mate were escorting their chick to the deck. After much fluttering, they all settled on the madrone twigs inches over my head; then Shadow and his mate looked at me, as if presenting their offspring for my appraisal.

Wonder of wonders! He was almost all albino. No chestnut color roamed his back, and only a partial dusty-gray skull cap topped his head.

"Well, I shall call you Whitey II," I said. Quickly I reached inside for a handful of sunflower seeds. I thought the youngster would find them easier eating than the harder peanuts and cashews. Holding out my hand, I waited for Shadow or his mate to take a seed for

167

Whitey II. Instead, they did not move and seemed somewhat uncomfortable when I looked at them.

Then Whitey II half-fell, half-fluttered down into my hand. Peering at the seeds, he selected one and then hopped onto my wrist. Still carrying the seed in his beak, he moved down my arm, raised to the tree, and perched upon my shoulder. As I turned my head to face him, with his beak he delicately placed the seed between my lips.

Whitey had returned. From far off in the forest came the cry of the wise old owl. "Who, who?"

Before I had not known, but now I knew his meaning.